Math 2

An Incremental Development

Student Workbook (Part Two)

Nancy Larson

with

Roseann Paolino

Saxon Publishers, Inc.

Math 2: An Incremental Development

Student Workbook

Copyright © 1997 by Saxon Publishers, Inc. and Nancy Larson

Printed in the United States of America

ISBN 13: 978-0-939798-82-7 (set)
ISBN 13: 978-1-56577-450-6 (wb.1)
ISBN 13: 978-1-56577-451-3 (wb. 2)

Editor: Deborah Williams
Production Supervisor: David Pond
Graphic Artists: Scott Kirby, John Chitwood, Gary Skidmore,
            Tim Maltz, and Chad Threet

35 0304 21
4500819023

Reaching us via the Internet

www.saxonpublishers.com

E-mail: info@saxonpublishers.com

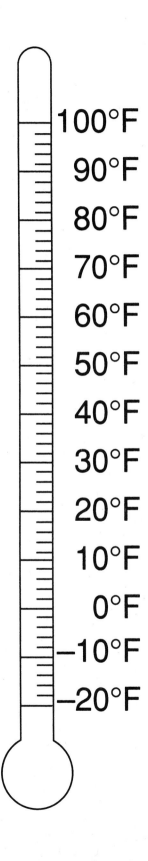

100°F
90°F
80°F
70°F
60°F
50°F
40°F
30°F
20°F
10°F
0°F
−10°F
−20°F

1.

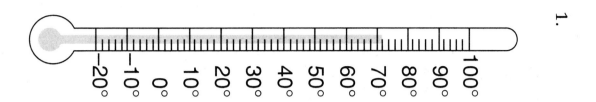

2.

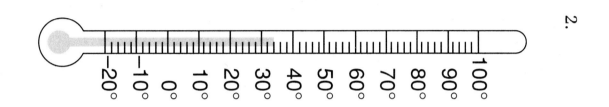

3.

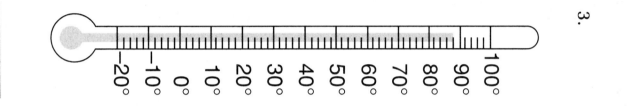

4.

28°

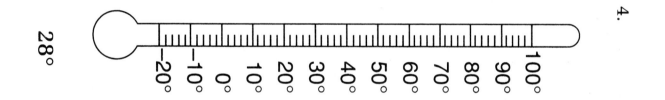

5.

46°

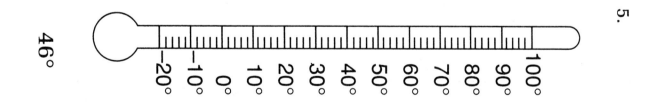

6.

74°

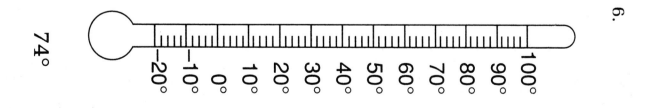

$$\begin{array}{r} 2 \\ +\ 8 \\ \hline \end{array} \qquad \begin{array}{r} 3 \\ +\ 5 \\ \hline \end{array} \qquad \begin{array}{r} 5 \\ +\ 6 \\ \hline \end{array} \qquad \begin{array}{r} 8 \\ +\ 3 \\ \hline \end{array} \qquad \begin{array}{r} 6 \\ +\ 8 \\ \hline \end{array}$$

11 or 108   11   11

$$\begin{array}{r} 3 \\ +\ 4 \\ \hline \end{array} \qquad \begin{array}{r} 7 \\ +\ 7 \\ \hline \end{array} \qquad \begin{array}{r} 1 \\ +\ 9 \\ \hline \end{array} \qquad \begin{array}{r} 6 \\ +\ 3 \\ \hline \end{array} \qquad \begin{array}{r} 4 \\ +\ 5 \\ \hline \end{array}$$

$$\begin{array}{r} 5 \\ +\ 7 \\ \hline \end{array} \qquad \begin{array}{r} 6 \\ +\ 9 \\ \hline \end{array} \qquad \begin{array}{r} 3 \\ +\ 4 \\ \hline \end{array} \qquad \begin{array}{r} 9 \\ +\ 9 \\ \hline \end{array} \qquad \begin{array}{r} 8 \\ +\ 5 \\ \hline \end{array}$$

$$\begin{array}{r} 6 \\ +\ 7 \\ \hline \end{array} \qquad \begin{array}{r} 7 \\ +\ 4 \\ \hline \end{array} \qquad \begin{array}{r} 8 \\ +\ 9 \\ \hline \end{array} \qquad \begin{array}{r} 3 \\ +\ 7 \\ \hline \end{array} \qquad \begin{array}{r} 5 \\ +\ 3 \\ \hline \end{array}$$

$$\begin{array}{r} 4 \\ +\ 4 \\ \hline \end{array} \qquad \begin{array}{r} 6 \\ +\ 5 \\ \hline \end{array} \qquad \begin{array}{r} 3 \\ +\ 6 \\ \hline \end{array} \qquad \begin{array}{r} 8 \\ +\ 3 \\ \hline \end{array} \qquad \begin{array}{r} 7 \\ +\ 6 \\ \hline \end{array}$$

Score: _____

Name __Avery__

Date __8/6 2021__

Write a number sentence for the story. Write the answer with a label.

1. Erin is on page thirty-five in the book she is reading. If she reads twenty more pages, what page will she be on then?

   Number sentence ___35 35 20 = L___   Answer ___55___

2. Write the fraction that tells how much is shaded.

   1/2   1/3   1/4

3. What is the temperature on the thermometer? ___54___ °F

4. I have **42¢**. What coins could I have?

   ___45 penes___

   What is another way to make **42¢**?

   ___8 neces and tow pen's___

5. Color the congruent shapes red.

6. Find the answers.

dimes	pennies
2	1
+ 2	3
44	8

dimes	pennies
5	4
+ 3	5
8	9

   $2 + 4 + 6 + 8 =$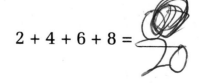

2-69Wa

Name _____

Date _____

Write a number sentence for the story. Write the answer with a label.

1. Stanley is on page forty in the book he is reading. If he reads fifteen more pages, what page will he be on then?

    Number sentence  Answer ___55___

2. Write the fraction that tells how much is shaded.

    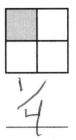 $\frac{1}{4}$

    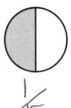 $\frac{1}{5}$

      $\frac{1}{3}$

3. What is the temperature on the thermometer? ___88___ °F

4. I have **45¢**. What coins could I have?

    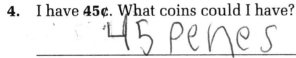 45 penes

    What is another way to make **45¢**?

     43   25   75

5. Color the congruent shapes red.

6. Find the answers.

dimes	pennies
3	6
+ 4	2
7	8

dimes	pennies
1	4
+ 7	4
8	8

    $1 + 3 + 5 + 7 + 9 =$ ___20___

Name _____

Date _____

Write a number sentence for the story. Write the answer with a label.

1. Phil had 7 dimes. He gave his brother 2 dimes. How many dimes does Phil have now?

   Number sentence ___ $7 - 2 = 5$ _____

   Answer ___ 5 ___   How much money is that? ___ 50 ¢ ___

2. Darlene has 4 pairs of mittens.
   Draw the mittens.
   How many mittens did you draw? ___ 8 ___

3. Show half past two on the clock.
   Write the digital time.

   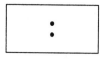

   It's morning. Circle
   the correct label.

   a.m.   p.m.

4. Draw a dozen eggs.

5. Find the answers.

   42 + 10 = _____   37 − 10 = _____

   58 − 10 = _____   29 + 10 = _____

   $\begin{array}{r} 4 \\ 7 \\ + 6 \\ \hline \end{array}$ $\begin{array}{r} 9 \\ 2 \\ 1 \\ + 8 \\ \hline \end{array}$

6. Put a dot inside each angle.
   Count the number of angles
   in each shape.

   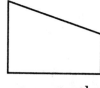

   _____ angles   _____ angles

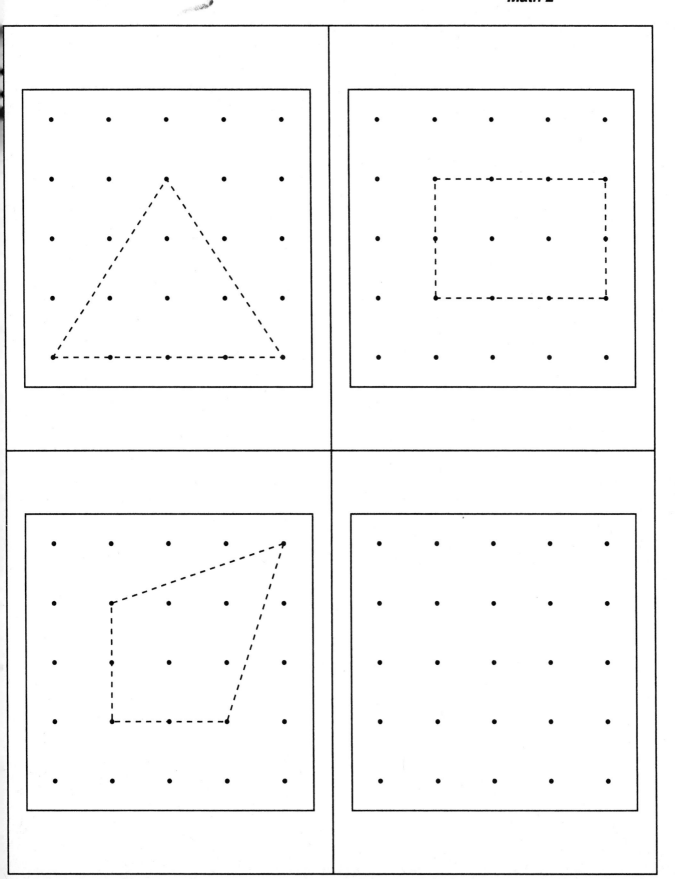

Name __Avery__   **LESSON 71A**
Date __9/22/2022__   *Math 2*

1. Mrs. Gustin put 3 pennies and 6 dimes in the coin cup.

    How much money is in the coin cup? __63__

    Andy took a dime out of the coin cup. How much money is in the coin cup now?

    Number sentence __63 - 10 = 53__   Answer __53__

2. Write the fraction that tells how much is shaded.

    $\dfrac{5}{6}$ $\dfrac{1}{8}$

3. Color the thermometer to show 38°F.

4. Fill in the children's names to show the ice cream flavors they like.

    Amy likes only chocolate.
    Chris likes vanilla and chocolate.
    Sue likes only vanilla.
    Bob likes only vanilla.
    Jim likes both flavors.

    ICE CREAM FLAVORS

    CHOCOLATE   VANILLA

    How many children like chocolate? _____

    How many children like vanilla? _____

5. Fill in the missing numbers on this piece of a hundred number chart.

    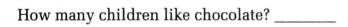

6. Find the answers.

    67 − 10 = _____   63 + 10 = _____   18 − 1 = _____

    10 less than 74 = _____   10 more than 41 = _____

1. Mrs. Trotter put 4 pennies and 3 dimes in the coin cup.

   How much money is in the coin cup? _____

   Brian took a penny out of the coin cup. How much money is in the coin cup now?

   Number sentence _____ Answer _____

2. Write the fraction that tells how much is shaded.

   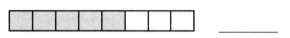 _____    _____

3. Color the thermometer to show 54°F.

4. Fill in the children's names to show the ice cream flavors they like.

   ICE CREAM FLAVORS

   CHOCOLATE   STRAWBERRY

   Mike likes only strawberry.
   Steve likes both flavors.
   Jim likes only chocolate.
   Mary likes both flavors.
   Lisa likes only strawberry.

   How many children like chocolate? _____

   How many children like strawberry? _____

5. Fill in the missing numbers on this piece of a hundred number chart.

   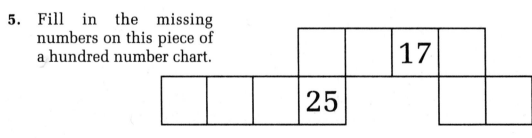

6. Find the answers.

   29 − 10 = _____   49 + 10 = _____   17 − 1 = _____

   10 less than 53 = _____   10 more than 27 = _____

Name _____

Name _____

Dimes   Pennies

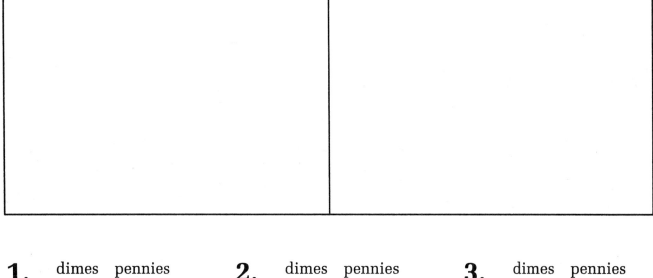

1. dimes   pennies

	dimes	pennies	
	4	3	¢
+	2	5	¢

2. dimes   pennies

	dimes	pennies	
	6	6	¢
+	1	8	¢

3. dimes   pennies

	dimes	pennies	
	4	9	¢
+	3	7	¢

4.
```
   4 4 ¢
 + 4 6 ¢
 ───────
```

5.
```
   6 5 ¢
 + 2 2 ¢
 ───────
```

6.
```
     8 ¢
 + 5 3 ¢
 ───────
```

9	2	6	5	0	9	7	1	2	5
+ 1	+ 2	+ 4	+ 1	+ 7	+ 9	+ 3	+ 6	+ 5	+ 4

9	2	8	4	6	7	3	9	0	4
+ 4	+ 0	+ 7	+ 1	+ 6	+ 8	+ 2	+ 8	+ 8	+ 6

5	3	0	8	3	7	7	1	6	2
+ 2	+ 9	+ 6	+ 1	+ 3	+ 4	+ 0	+ 5	+ 7	+ 3

1	5	7	3	2	9	7	4	0	6
+ 0	+ 5	+ 6	+ 4	+ 6	+ 5	+ 2	+ 9	+ 3	+ 8

8	3	1	0	6	5	1	8	2	5
+ 2	+ 5	+ 7	+ 0	+ 2	+ 7	+ 4	+ 6	+ 9	+ 0

6	0	3	4	9	1	6	2	8	0
+ 3	+ 5	+ 7	+ 4	+ 2	+ 8	+ 5	+ 4	+ 8	+ 9

4	7	9	9	5	0	3	7	6	4
+ 2	+ 7	+ 0	+ 6	+ 8	+ 1	+ 6	+ 9	+ 0	+ 8

7	2	4	1	4	8	3	8	1	5
+ 1	+ 6	+ 7	+ 2	+ 5	+ 9	+ 0	+ 3	+ 9	+ 6

1	3	0	5	9	2	8	4	6	1
+ 1	+ 8	+ 2	+ 9	+ 3	+ 7	+ 0	+ 3	+ 9	+ 3

8	4	5	2	3	7	9	0	8	6
+ 5	+ 0	+ 3	+ 8	+ 1	+ 5	+ 7	+ 4	+ 4	+ 1

Name _____

Date _____

1. Curtis had 15 dimes. He gave 9 dimes to his sister. How many dimes does he have now?

    Number sentence _____ Answer _____

    How much money is that? _____

2. Color the thermometer to show 26°F.

3. How much money is this? _____

4. Find the answers.

    7 + 2 + 8 + 1 + 3 = _____   ten more than 26 = _____

    6 + 6 + 4 + 2 = _____   ten less than 47 = _____

    42 − 10 = _____   1 less than 12 = _____

5. It's evening. What time is it?

    Answer _____

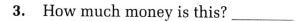

6. Write a fraction that tells how much is shaded.

    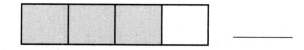   _____

Name _____

Date _____

1. Shelley had 13 nickels. She gave 9 nickels to her brother. How many nickels does she have now?

   Number sentence _____ Answer _____

   How much money is that? _____

2. Color the thermometer to show 28°F.

3. How much money is this? _____

4. Find the answers.

   5 + 6 + 3 + 5 + 7 = _____   ten more than 86 = _____

   7 + 7 + 3 + 1 = _____   ten less than 53 = _____

   38 − 10 = _____   1 less than 14 = _____

5. It's morning. What time is it?

   Answer _____

6. Write a fraction that tells how much is shaded.

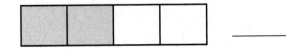 _____

1. Write a some, some more story using the numbers 5 and 3.

   _____

   _____

   Write a question for the story.

   _____

   Write a number sentence and find the answer.

   Number sentence _____ Answer _____

2. Write these numbers in order from least to greatest.

   | 49 25 63 28 42 | ____ ____ ____ ____ ____

   least   greatest

3. Draw 7 pairs of shoes. How many shoes is that? _____

4. Color the congruent shapes red.

   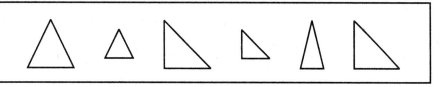

5. Use dimes and pennies to find the answers.

dimes	pennies	
5	4	¢
2	8	¢

dimes	pennies	
3	9	¢
2	1	¢

dimes	pennies	
2	4	¢
6	3	¢

Name _____

Date _____

1. Write a some, some more story using the numbers 8 and 4.

_____

_____

Write a question for the story.

_____

Write a number sentence and find the answer.

Number sentence _____ Answer _____

2. Write these numbers in order from least to greatest.

| 53 71 37 58 33 |

____ ____ ____ ____ ____
least   greatest

3. Draw 6 pairs of gloves. How many gloves is that? _____

4. Color the congruent shapes red.

5. Use dimes and pennies to find the answers.

dimes	pennies
5	4	¢
1	5	¢
+		

dimes	pennies
2	8	¢
1	3	¢
+		

dimes	pennies
2	6	¢
5	4	¢
+		

Draw these line segments.

3"　•

$2\frac{1}{2}$"　•

$1\frac{1}{2}$"　•

$\frac{1}{2}$"　•

$4\frac{1}{2}$"　•

Measure these line segments.

1. •————————————•

2. •————————————————————•

3. •————————•

4. •——————————•

5. •——•

12 − 9	17 − 9	11 − 9	10 − 9	15 − 9
9 − 9	13 − 9	16 − 9	12 − 9	14 − 9
18 − 9	13 − 9	9 − 9	15 − 9	11 − 9
10 − 9	17 − 9	14 − 9	12 − 9	13 − 9
16 − 9	11 − 9	18 − 9	15 − 9	12 − 9

Score: _____

Name _____ **LESSON 74A**
                                                Math 2
Date _____

1. Write a some, some went away story using the numbers 10 and 6.

   _____

   _____

   Write a question for the story.

   _____

   Write a number sentence and find the answer.

   Number sentence _____

   Answer _____

2. What temperature is shown on the thermometer? _____°F

3. Use your ruler to draw these line segments.

   $3\frac{1}{2}''$ •

   $1\frac{1}{2}''$ •

4. Find the answers.

16	12	17
− 9	− 9	− 9

	2	8	¢
+	3	1	¢

	1	4	¢
+	3	3	¢

5. Use the graph to answer the questions.

   How many children's names are on this graph? _____

   How many children like chocolate ice cream? _____

   How many children like both
   vanilla and chocolate ice cream? _____

   Which flavor does Carol like? _____

   ICE CREAM FLAVORS

   VANILLA   CHOCOLATE

   Carol   Jan
        Mike   Phil
   Pat   Zed

Name _____

Date _____

1. Write a some, some went away story using the numbers 7 and 5.

   _____

   _____

   Write a question for the story.

   _____

   Write a number sentence and find the answer.

   Number sentence _____

   Answer _____

2. What temperature is shown on the thermometer? _____°F

3. Finish the number patterns.

   20, 22, 24, 26, _____ , _____ , _____ , _____ , _____

   50, 45, 40, 35, _____ , _____ , _____ , _____ , _____

4. Find the answers.

   $$\begin{array}{r} 14 \\ -\ 9 \\ \hline \end{array} \qquad \begin{array}{r} 11 \\ -\ 9 \\ \hline \end{array} \qquad \begin{array}{r} 15 \\ -\ 9 \\ \hline \end{array}$$

2	7	¢
+ 4	1	¢

3	5	¢
+ 5	0	¢

100°F
90°F
80°F
70°F
60°F
50°F
40°F
30°F
20°F
10°F
0°F
–10°F
–20°F

5. Use the graph to answer the questions.

   How many children like vanilla ice cream? _____

   Which flavor does Phil like? _____

   Which flavors does Mike like? _____

   _____

   ICE CREAM FLAVORS

   VANILLA   CHOCOLATE

   Carol

   Pat   Mike

   Jan

   Phil

   Zed

Name _____

Date _____

1. There were a dozen cupcakes in the box. Sara, Bill, and Peter each ate one cupcake. How many cupcakes are left?

   Number sentence _____   Answer _____

2. Use the graph to answer the following questions.

   How many children's names are on this graph? _____

   How many children like peas? _____

   How many children like squash? _____

   How many children like both peas and squash? _____

   Which vegetable does Jim like? _____

   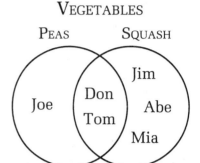

   VEGETABLES

3. How much money is this? _____

4. Find the answers.

   53 + 10 = _____   26 − 10 = _____   10 + 29 = _____

   10 more than 82 = _____   one less than 30 = _____

   6 + 3 + 9 + 2 + 7 + 1 = _____   10 less than 63 = _____

5. Circle the shape that is congruent to the shape on the left.

   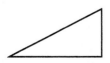   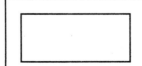   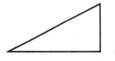

8	5	2	10	6
− 2	− 2	− 2	− 2	− 2

7	3	11	9	4
− 2	− 2	− 2	− 2	− 2

11	2	7	4	10
− 2	− 2	− 2	− 2	− 2

6	8	3	9	5
− 2	− 2	− 2	− 2	− 2

8	7	5	11	4
− 2	− 2	− 2	− 2	− 2

Score: _____

1. David has 7 dimes and 3 pennies. John has 5 pennies and 2 dimes. How much money do the two boys have altogether?

   Number sentence _____   Answer _____

2. Use your ruler to draw these line segments.

   $2\frac{1}{2}"$ •

   $\frac{1}{2}"$ •

3. Write the numbers that are ten less and ten more.

   _____ , 30, _____   _____ , 59, _____   _____ , 73, _____

4.
Divide the rectangle in half using a horizontal line segment.	Divide the rectangle in half using a vertical line segment.	Divide the rectangle in half using an oblique line segment.

   Color one half.   Color $\frac{1}{2}$.   Color $\frac{1}{2}$.

5. Find the answers.

   6 + 2 + 3 + 8 + 1 + 7 = _____   5 + 4 + 5 + 3 + 7 + 2 = _____

6. Finish the number patterns.

   _____ , _____ , _____ , 50, 60, 70, _____ , _____ , _____

   100, 110, 120, _____ , _____ , _____ , _____ , _____ , _____

   _____ , _____ , _____ , 18, 17, 16, _____ , _____ , _____

Name _____

Date _____

1. Linda has 4 dimes and 8 pennies. Amanda has 1 penny and 3 dimes. How much money do the two girls have altogether?

   Number sentence _____ Answer _____

2. Find the answers.

   $17 - 9 =$ _____ $15 - 9 =$ _____ $14 - 9 =$ _____

   $13 - 9 =$ _____ $12 - 9 =$ _____ $16 - 9 =$ _____

3. Write the numbers that are ten less and ten more.

   _____ , 20, _____   _____ , 43, _____   _____ , 68, _____

4. Divide the square in half using an oblique line segment.

   Color one half.

   Divide the square in half using a vertical line segment.

   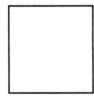

   Color $\frac{1}{2}$.

   Divide the square in half using a horizontal line segment.

   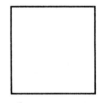

   Color $\frac{1}{2}$.

5. Find the answers.

   $2 + 3 + 9 + 7 + 5 + 1 =$ _____ $6 + 2 + 6 + 3 + 4 + 8 =$ _____

6. Finish the number patterns.

   _____ , _____ , _____ , 60, 50, 40, _____ , _____ , _____

   200, 210, 220, _____ , _____ , _____ , _____ , _____ , _____

   _____ , _____ , _____ , 26, 25, 24, _____ , _____ , _____

1.

12¢ + 29¢

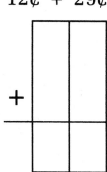

2.

55¢ + 26¢

3.

73¢ + 15¢

4.

29¢ + 21¢

5.

49¢ + 24¢

+
_____

6.

52¢ + 24¢

+
_____

7.

65¢ + 25¢

+
_____

8.

16¢ + 24¢

+
_____

9.

9¢ + 38¢

+
_____

10.

46¢ + 7¢

+
_____

3 − 2	6 − 1	5 − 0	7 − 2	8 − 4
6 − 6	8 − 2	9 − 1	14 − 7	9 − 2
16 − 8	3 − 0	4 − 2	5 − 1	11 − 2
8 − 0	12 − 6	5 − 2	3 − 1	6 − 3
10 − 2	18 − 9	7 − 1	6 − 2	7 − 7

Score: _____

2-76Fa

1. One of these is my favorite day of the week. Cross out the days of the week that cannot be my favorite day of the week.
It is not the sixth day of the week.
It is not a weekend day.
It does not begin with a T.
It is not the day that is in the middle of the week.

What is my favorite day? _____

Sunday
Monday
Tuesday
Wednesday
Thursday
Friday
Saturday

2. Draw a shape with 4 angles. How many sides does the shape have? _____

3. Write fractions that show how much is shaded.

 _____   _____   _____

4. Write the numbers that are one less and one more than each number.

_____ , 12, _____   _____ , 40, _____   _____ , 79, _____

5. Use your ruler to measure these line segments.

_____ "

_____ "

6. Find the answers.

39 − 10 = _____   6 + 3 + 2 + 4 + 8 + 1 = _____   4 7 ¢

                                                                              + 1 6 ¢
                                                                              _____

10 more than 52 = _____   10 less than 41 = _____

Name _____

Date _____

1. One of these is my brother's favorite day of the week. Cross out the days of the week that cannot be my brother's favorite day of the week.
It is not the first or the third day of the week.
It does not have 6 letters.
It is not the last day of the week.
It is not the day in the middle of the week.

   What is my brother's favorite day? _____

Sunday
Monday
Tuesday
Wednesday
Thursday
Friday
Saturday

2. Draw a shape with 3 angles. How many sides does the shape have? _____

3. Write fractions that show how much is shaded.

    _____    _____   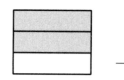 _____

4. Write the numbers that are one less and one more than each number.

   _____ , 16, _____   _____ , 29, _____   _____ , 60, _____

5. What is the best estimate of the length of this paper?

   5 inches   28 inches   11 inches   20 inches

6. Find the answers.

   84 − 10 = _____   9 + 3 + 1 + 4 + 7 = _____   6 7 ¢
                                                          + 2 3 ¢
                                                          _____

   10 more than 72 = _____   10 less than 63 = _____

1. Color 2½ squares

2. Color 3½ circles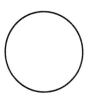

3. Color 4¼ squares

4. Color 1¾ circles

Write a mixed number to show how much is shaded.

5. _____

6. _____

7. _____

8. _____

12 − 9	17 − 9	11 − 9	10 − 9	15 − 9
9 − 9	13 − 9	16 − 9	12 − 9	14 − 9
18 − 9	13 − 9	9 − 9	15 − 9	11 − 9
10 − 9	17 − 9	14 − 9	12 − 9	13 − 9
16 − 9	11 − 9	18 − 9	15 − 9	12 − 9

Score: _____

2-77Fa

Name •
    (Draw a 4-inch line segment.)

Date •
    (Draw a $4\frac{1}{2}$-inch line segment.)

1. Theresa has 4 dimes and 7 pennies. Jennifer has 3 dimes and 12 pennies. How much money does each girl have?

    Theresa _____   Jennifer _____

    Who has the most money? _____

2. Color the thermometer to show 84°F.

3. Use your ruler to measure these line segments.

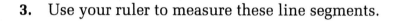 _____"

 _____"

4. It's morning. What time is it?

    Answer _____

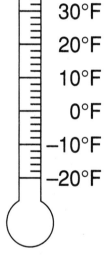

5. Color $3\frac{1}{2}$ circles.

6. Find the answers.

$$
\begin{array}{r} 4\,3\;¢ \\ +\,1\,7\;¢ \\ \hline \end{array}
\qquad
\begin{array}{r} 3\,7\;¢ \\ +\,5\,7\;¢ \\ \hline \end{array}
\qquad
\begin{array}{r} 2\,4\;¢ \\ +\,6\,5\;¢ \\ \hline \end{array}
\qquad
\begin{array}{r} 1\,6\;¢ \\ +\,3\,9\;¢ \\ \hline \end{array}
$$

1. Anita has 1 dime and 15 pennies. Christa has 2 dimes and 4 pennies. How much money does each girl have?

   Anita _____   Christa _____

   Who has the most money? _____

2. Color the thermometer to show 68°F.

3. Draw a dozen cookies.
   Daniel ate a half dozen.
   Put an X on the cookies he ate.

4. It's afternoon. What time is it?

   Answer _____

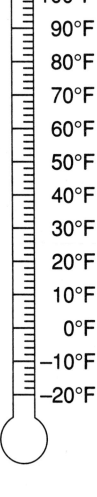

5. Color $2\frac{1}{2}$ squares.

6. Find the answers.

3 7 ¢	4 1 ¢	2 7 ¢	5 9 ¢
+ 1 5 ¢	+ 2 9 ¢	+ 5 2 ¢	+ 2 3 ¢

9 + 1	2 + 2	6 + 4	5 + 1	0 + 7	9 + 9	7 + 3	1 + 6	2 + 5	5 + 4
9 + 4	2 + 0	8 + 7	4 + 1	6 + 6	7 + 8	3 + 2	9 + 8	0 + 8	4 + 6
5 + 2	3 + 9	0 + 6	8 + 1	3 + 3	7 + 4	7 + 0	1 + 5	6 + 7	2 + 3
1 + 0	5 + 5	7 + 6	3 + 4	2 + 6	9 + 5	7 + 2	4 + 9	0 + 3	6 + 8
8 + 2	3 + 5	1 + 7	0 + 0	6 + 2	5 + 7	1 + 4	8 + 6	2 + 9	5 + 0
6 + 3	0 + 5	3 + 7	4 + 4	9 + 2	1 + 8	6 + 5	2 + 4	8 + 8	0 + 9
4 + 2	7 + 7	9 + 0	9 + 6	5 + 8	0 + 1	3 + 6	7 + 9	6 + 0	4 + 8
7 + 1	2 + 6	4 + 7	1 + 2	4 + 5	8 + 9	3 + 0	8 + 3	1 + 9	5 + 6
1 + 1	3 + 8	0 + 2	5 + 9	9 + 3	2 + 7	8 + 0	4 + 3	6 + 9	1 + 3
8 + 5	4 + 0	5 + 3	2 + 8	3 + 1	7 + 5	9 + 7	0 + 4	8 + 4	6 + 1

2-78Fa

Name •
(Draw a 3-inch line segment.)

Date •
(Draw a $3\frac{1}{2}$-inch line segment.)

1. Ryan and David each ate 5 marshmallows. Michael ate 2 marshmallows. How many marshmallows did the 3 boys eat altogether?

   Number sentence _____

   Answer _____

2. Write these numbers in order from least to greatest.

   | 321   114   259   170 |

   _____ _____ _____ _____
   least   greatest

3. One of these is my favorite number.
   Cross out the numbers that cannot be my favorite number.
   It has 2 digits.
   It is between 80 and 100.
   It is not an odd number.
   What is my favorite number? _____

   | 98 |
   | 32 |
   | 127 |
   | 83 |
   | 9 |

4. Write the examples vertically. Find the answers.

   74¢ + 9¢   17¢ + 48¢   44¢ + 36¢   82¢ + 16¢

   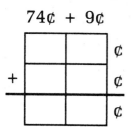
   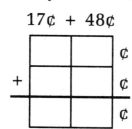
   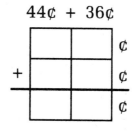

5. Fill in the missing numbers in the number patterns.

   _____ , _____ , _____ , 35, 40, 45, _____ , _____ , _____

   15, 17, 19, _____ , _____ , _____ , _____ , _____ , _____

2-78Wa

Date _____

1. Joe and Robert each ate 3 pieces of watermelon. Collin ate 4 pieces of watermelon. How many pieces of watermelon did the 3 boys eat altogether?

   Number sentence _____

   Answer _____

2. Write these numbers in order from least to greatest.

   | 148   220   171   205 |

   _____ _____ _____ _____

   least   greatest

3. One of these is my brother's favorite number.
   Cross out the numbers that cannot be his favorite number.
   It does not have 3 digits.
   It is between 10 and 30.
   It is not an odd number.
   What is my brother's favorite number? _____

   148
   24
   15
   38
   82

4. Write the examples vertically. Find the answers.

   51¢ + 16¢   7¢ + 37¢   55¢ + 29¢   14¢ + 36¢

   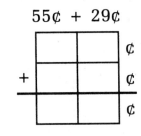   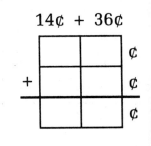

5. Fill in the missing numbers in the number patterns.

   70, 65, 60, _____ , _____ , _____ , _____ , _____ , _____

   12, 14, 16, _____ , _____ , _____ , _____ , _____ , _____

Name •
(Draw a 2-inch line segment.)

Date •
(Draw a $2\frac{1}{2}$-inch line segment.)

1. There are 17 children in Room 12. Nine children went to the nurse's office to have their eyes checked. How many children are in Room 12 now?

Number sentence _____

Answer _____

2. Write these numbers in order from least to greatest.

291	67	134	178

_____ _____ _____ _____
least   greatest

3. Color the thermometer to show 44°F.

4. Draw a picture to show 251. (Use ☐ for 100, ☐ for 10, ☐ for 1.)

5. Color $2\frac{3}{4}$ circles.

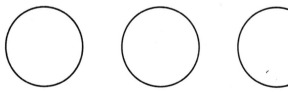

6. Write the examples vertically. Find the answers.

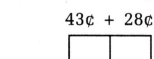
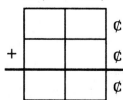

43¢ + 28¢   31¢ + 9¢   52¢ + 13¢

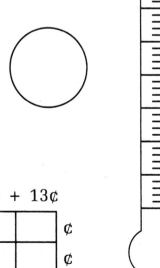

1. There are 15 children in Room 17. Nine children left to go to the library. How many children are in Room 17 now?

    Number sentence _____

    Answer _____

2. Write these numbers in order from least to greatest.

    | 152   212   73   243 |

    _____   _____   _____   _____

    least   greatest

3. Color the thermometer to show 56°F.

4. Draw a picture to show 143. (Use 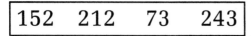 for 100, ⬚ for 10, ☐ for 1.)

5. Color $1\frac{1}{4}$ squares.

          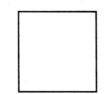

6. Write the examples vertically. Find the answers.

    62¢ + 27¢   17¢ + 45¢   8¢ + 86¢

    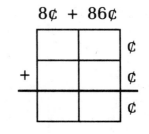

100°F
90°F
80°F
70°F
60°F
50°F
40°F
30°F
20°F
10°F
0°F
−10°F
−20°F

1. Ryan has 5 dimes and 7 pennies. How much money does he have? _____

   Daniel has 3 dimes and 2 pennies. How much money does he have? _____

   How much money do the two boys have altogether?

   Number sentence _____   Answer _____

2. Write these numbers in order from least to greatest.

   | 48   27   25   43   39 | _____ _____ _____ _____ _____
                                least   greatest

3. Write the fractions that show what part is shaded.

   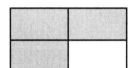 _____   _____

4. Draw a dozen donuts. Color a half dozen brown to show that they are chocolate.

   How many donuts are chocolate? _____

   How many donuts are not chocolate? _____

5. Add.

   $6 + 4 + 7 + 2 + 3 + 1 =$ _____

   $$\begin{array}{r} 2\,4\,¢ \\ +\ 5\,3\,¢ \\ \hline \end{array}$$ $$\begin{array}{r} 1\,6\,¢ \\ +\ 7\,2\,¢ \\ \hline \end{array}$$

How many squares and triangles can you find in each design?

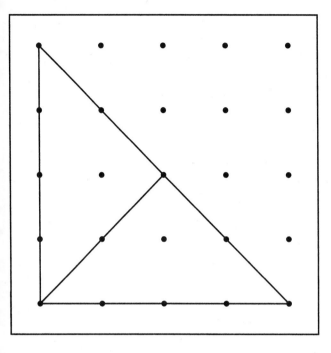

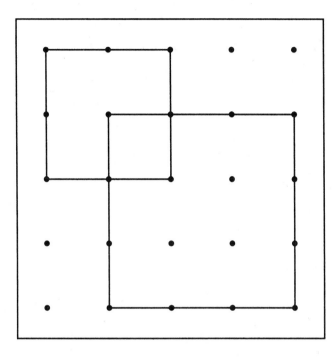

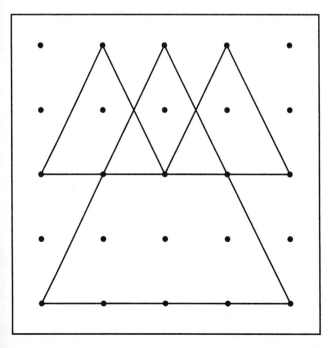

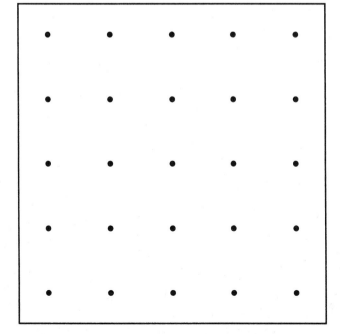

Name •

(Draw a 3-inch line segment.)

Date •

(Draw a $3\frac{1}{2}$-inch line segment.)

1. Draw 5 apples. Divide each apple in half.

How many pieces of apple do you have? _____

2. What number does this picture show? _____

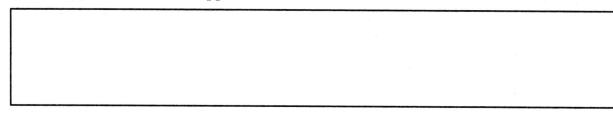

3. Write these numbers in order from least to greatest.

| 249 434 193 216 180 |

_____   _____   _____   _____   _____

least   greatest

4. I have 3 dimes, 2 nickels, and 4 pennies. Draw the coins.

How much money is this? _____

5. Find the answers.

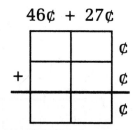

46¢ + 27¢

35¢ + 55¢

21¢ + 48¢

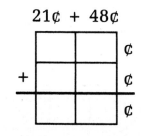

Name _____   **LESSON 81B**

Date _____   **Math 2**

1. Draw 4 bananas. Divide each banana in half.

   [   ]

   How many pieces of banana do you have? _____

2. What number does this picture show? _____

   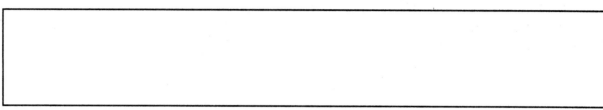

3. Write these numbers in order from least to greatest.

   | 273 192 154 337 230 | _____ _____ _____ _____ _____

   least   greatest

4. I have 5 dimes, 3 nickels, and 1 penny. Draw the coins.

   [   ]

   How much money is this? _____

5. Find the answers.

   53¢ + 36¢   29¢ + 17¢   48¢ + 22¢

   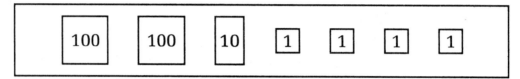
   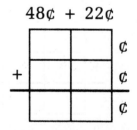

Name ________________________________

MASTER 2-82

Math 2

4 9 5	8 6 2
9 2 ☐	8 9 ☐

2-82Ma

9 + 1	2 + 2	6 + 4	5 + 1	0 + 7	9 + 9	7 + 3	1 + 6	2 + 5	5 + 4
9 + 4	2 + 0	8 + 7	4 + 1	6 + 6	7 + 8	3 + 2	9 + 8	0 + 8	4 + 6
5 + 2	3 + 9	0 + 6	8 + 1	3 + 3	7 + 4	7 + 0	1 + 5	6 + 7	2 + 3
1 + 0	5 + 5	7 + 6	3 + 4	2 + 6	9 + 5	7 + 2	4 + 9	0 + 3	6 + 8
8 + 2	3 + 5	1 + 7	0 + 0	6 + 2	5 + 7	1 + 4	8 + 6	2 + 9	5 + 0
6 + 3	0 + 5	3 + 7	4 + 4	9 + 2	1 + 8	6 + 5	2 + 4	8 + 8	0 + 9
4 + 2	7 + 7	9 + 0	9 + 6	5 + 8	0 + 1	3 + 6	7 + 9	6 + 0	4 + 8
7 + 1	2 + 6	4 + 7	1 + 2	4 + 5	8 + 9	3 + 0	8 + 3	1 + 9	5 + 6
1 + 1	3 + 8	0 + 2	5 + 9	9 + 3	2 + 7	8 + 0	4 + 3	6 + 9	1 + 3
8 + 5	4 + 0	5 + 3	2 + 8	3 + 1	7 + 5	9 + 7	0 + 4	8 + 4	6 + 1

Name •

(Draw a 4-inch line segment.)

Date •

(Draw a $4\frac{1}{2}$-inch line segment.)

1. Fifteen grade 2 children rode bicycles to school. Seventeen grade 3 children rode bicycles to school. How many children in grades 2 and 3 rode bicycles to school?

   Number sentence _____ Answer _____

2. Write the fact family number sentences for 2, 4, and 6.

   _____   _____

   _____   _____

3. Write a mixed number to show how much is shaded. _____

4. Show half past two on the clocks.

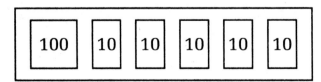

5. What number does this picture show? _____

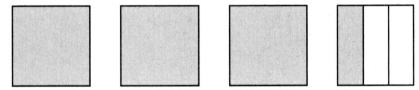

| 100 | 10 | 10 | 10 | 10 | 10 |

6. Find the answers.

   $\begin{array}{r} 5\,8\ ¢ \\ +\ 1\,6\ ¢ \\ \hline \end{array}$ $\begin{array}{r} 9\ ¢ \\ +\ 4\,2\ ¢ \\ \hline \end{array}$ $\begin{array}{r} 3\,6\ ¢ \\ +\ 5\,1\ ¢ \\ \hline \end{array}$

2-82Wa

Name _____

Date _____

1. Twelve children in Room 16 ride the bus to school. The other nine children in Room 16 walk to school. How many children are in Room 16?

   Number sentence _____   Answer _____

2. Write the fact family number sentences for 3, 5, and 8.

   _____   _____

   _____   _____

3. Write a mixed number to show how much is shaded. _____

4. Show half past eight on the clocks.

   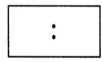   

5. What number does this picture show? _____

   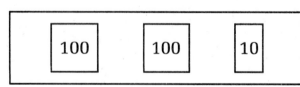

6. Find the answers.

$$\begin{array}{r} 23¢ \\ + \ 48¢ \\ \hline \end{array} \qquad \begin{array}{r} 8¢ \\ + \ 29¢ \\ \hline \end{array} \qquad \begin{array}{r} 52¢ \\ + \ 31¢ \\ \hline \end{array}$$

$$
\begin{array}{r} 4 \\ -\ 3 \\ \hline \end{array}
\qquad
\begin{array}{r} 11 \\ -\ 2 \\ \hline \end{array}
\qquad
\begin{array}{r} 8 \\ -\ 7 \\ \hline \end{array}
\qquad
\begin{array}{r} 16 \\ -\ 7 \\ \hline \end{array}
\qquad
\begin{array}{r} 6 \\ -\ 4 \\ \hline \end{array}
$$

$$
\begin{array}{r} 10 \\ -\ 8 \\ \hline \end{array}
\qquad
\begin{array}{r} 8 \\ -\ 6 \\ \hline \end{array}
\qquad
\begin{array}{r} 6 \\ -\ 5 \\ \hline \end{array}
\qquad
\begin{array}{r} 12 \\ -\ 3 \\ \hline \end{array}
\qquad
\begin{array}{r} 5 \\ -\ 4 \\ \hline \end{array}
$$

$$
\begin{array}{r} 13 \\ -\ 4 \\ \hline \end{array}
\qquad
\begin{array}{r} 7 \\ -\ 6 \\ \hline \end{array}
\qquad
\begin{array}{r} 5 \\ -\ 3 \\ \hline \end{array}
\qquad
\begin{array}{r} 9 \\ -\ 8 \\ \hline \end{array}
\qquad
\begin{array}{r} 15 \\ -\ 6 \\ \hline \end{array}
$$

$$
\begin{array}{r} 7 \\ -\ 5 \\ \hline \end{array}
\qquad
\begin{array}{r} 11 \\ -\ 2 \\ \hline \end{array}
\qquad
\begin{array}{r} 14 \\ -\ 5 \\ \hline \end{array}
\qquad
\begin{array}{r} 9 \\ -\ 7 \\ \hline \end{array}
\qquad
\begin{array}{r} 17 \\ -\ 8 \\ \hline \end{array}
$$

$$
\begin{array}{r} 8 \\ -\ 6 \\ \hline \end{array}
\qquad
\begin{array}{r} 5 \\ -\ 4 \\ \hline \end{array}
\qquad
\begin{array}{r} 16 \\ -\ 7 \\ \hline \end{array}
\qquad
\begin{array}{r} 7 \\ -\ 6 \\ \hline \end{array}
\qquad
\begin{array}{r} 10 \\ -\ 1 \\ \hline \end{array}
$$

Score: _____

Name •

(Draw a 2-inch line segment.)

Date •

(Draw a $2\frac{1}{2}$-inch line segment.)

1. David has a new box of 48 crayons. He gave Bobby 10 crayons to use. How many crayons does David have now?

Number sentence _____ Answer _____

2. Draw a picture to show 235. (Use ☐ for 100, ☐ for 10, ☐ for 1.)

3. What temperature is shown on the thermometer? _____°F

4. Fill in the missing numbers on this piece of a hundred number chart.

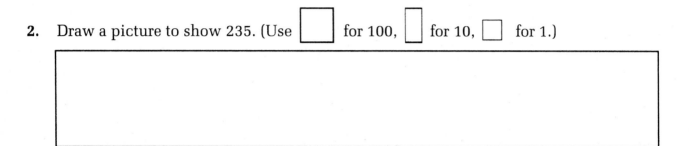

5. Write the fact family number sentences for 5, 9, and 14.

_____   _____

_____   _____

6. Find the answers.

$$25¢ + 48¢ \qquad 16¢ + 48¢ \qquad 24¢ + 32¢$$

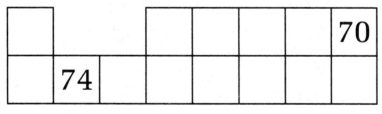

Name _____

Date _____

1. Melanie had a new set of 24 markers. She gave Scott 10 markers to use. How many markers does Melanie have now?

   Number sentence _____ Answer _____

2. Draw a picture to show 142. (Use ☐ for 100, ☐ for 10, ☐ for 1.)

3. What temperature is shown on the thermometer? _____°F

4. Fill in the missing numbers on this piece of a hundred number chart.

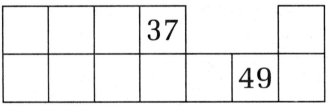

5. Write the fact family number sentences for 7, 9, and 16.

   _____   _____

   _____   _____

6. Find the answers.

   61¢ + 18¢   32¢ + 29¢   53¢ + 17¢

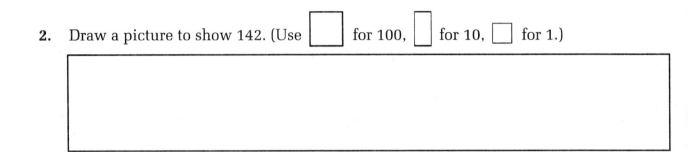

100°F
90°F
80°F
70°F
60°F
50°F
40°F
30°F
20°F
10°F
0°F
−10°F
−20°F

Write the time.	Write the time.	Write the time.

:	:	:

Show the time.	Show the time.	Show the time.
2:45	**8:05**	**4:50**

4	11	8	16	6
− 3	− 2	− 7	− 7	− 4

10	8	6	12	5
− 8	− 6	− 5	− 3	− 4

13	7	5	9	15
− 4	− 6	− 3	− 8	− 6

7	11	14	9	17
− 5	− 2	− 5	− 7	− 8

8	5	16	7	10
− 6	− 4	− 7	− 6	− 1

Score: _____

Name ●
(Draw a 4-inch line segment.)

Date ●
(Draw a 4½-inch line segment.)

1. Forty children chose chocolate. Thirty-seven children chose vanilla. How many children is this altogether?

   Number sentence _____ Answer _____

   What was the favorite flavor? _____

2. Draw a picture to show 361. (Use ☐ for 100, ☐ for 10, ☐ for 1.)

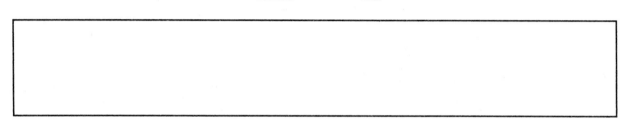

3. Measure each line segment.

   horizontal line segment _____"

   oblique line segment _____"

   vertical line segment _____"

4. Write the fact family number sentences for 3, 7, and 10.

   _____   _____

   _____   _____

5. It's afternoon. What time is it? _____

6. Find the answers.

$$
\begin{array}{r} 3\,5\,¢ \\ +\ 1\,6\,¢ \\ \hline \end{array}
\qquad
\begin{array}{r} 4\,7\,¢ \\ +\ 4\,7\,¢ \\ \hline \end{array}
\qquad
\begin{array}{r} 1\,1\,¢ \\ +\ 3\,9\,¢ \\ \hline \end{array}
\qquad
\begin{array}{r} 5\,1\,¢ \\ +\ 2\,8\,¢ \\ \hline \end{array}
$$

1. Twenty children chose strawberry. Fifty-one children chose peach. How many children is this altogether?

   Number sentence _____ Answer _____

   What was the favorite flavor? _____

2. Draw a picture to show 432. (Use ☐ for 100, ☐ for 10, ☐ for 1.)

3. Find the answers.

16	14	11	17	15	8	5	9	6	7
− 9	− 9	− 9	− 9	− 9	− 2	− 2	− 2	− 2	− 2

4. Write the fact family number sentences for 2, 8, and 10.

   _____   _____

   _____   _____

5. It's morning. What time is it? _____

6. Find the answers.

$$32¢ + 17¢ \qquad 28¢ + 28¢ \qquad 9¢ + 45¢ \qquad 62¢ + 36¢$$

_____
+ _____
_____

Total _____

_____
+ _____
_____

Total _____

_____
+ _____
_____

Total _____

_____

_____
+ _____
_____

Total _____

_____

_____
+ _____
_____

Total _____

_____

_____
+ _____
_____

Total _____

4 − 3	11 − 2	8 − 7	16 − 7	6 − 4
10 − 8	8 − 6	6 − 5	12 − 3	5 − 4
13 − 4	7 − 6	5 − 3	9 − 8	15 − 6
7 − 5	11 − 2	14 − 5	9 − 7	17 − 8
8 − 6	5 − 4	16 − 7	7 − 6	10 − 1

Score: _____

Name •
(Draw a 2-inch line segment.)

Date •
(Draw a 2½-inch line segment.)

1. There were 17 children in Room 5. Eight children went to the library. How many children are in Room 5 now?

Number sentence _____ Answer _____

2. What number does this picture show? _____

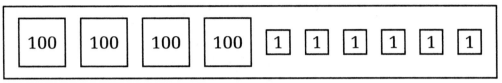

3. Draw two dozen eggs.
   Color a half dozen red.
   How many eggs are not colored?

   Answer _____

4. Write the numbers that are 10 less and 10 more.

   _____ , 60, _____   _____ , 35, _____   _____ , 47, _____

5. Write these numbers in order from least to greatest.

   | 129 243 170 260 259 | ____ ____ ____ ____ ____
                                    least   greatest

6. Show 5:35 on the clock face.

7. Find the answers.

1 6 ¢	2 7 ¢	
2 2 ¢	3 1 ¢	6 9 ¢
+ 4 8 ¢	+ 1 3 ¢	+ 1 7 ¢

Name _____

Date _____

1. There were 15 children in a swimming pool. Six children climbed out of the pool. How many children are in the pool now?

   Number sentence _____ Answer _____

2. What number does this picture show? _____

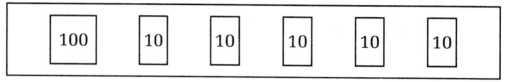

3. Draw two dozen cookies.
   Color a half dozen brown.
   How many cookies are not colored?

   Answer _____

4. Write the numbers that are 10 less and 10 more.

   _____ , 80, _____   _____ , 55, _____   _____ , 39, _____

5. Write these numbers in order from least to greatest.

   | 285 123 244 110 229 | _____ _____ _____ _____ _____

   least   greatest

6. Show 8:25 on the clock face.

7. Find the answers.

   $$\begin{array}{r} 1\,3\,¢ \\ 4\,2\,¢ \\ +\,4\,1\,¢ \\ \hline \end{array} \qquad \begin{array}{r} 2\,4\,¢ \\ 1\,1\,¢ \\ +\,3\,3\,¢ \\ \hline \end{array} \qquad \begin{array}{r} 6\,9\,¢ \\ +\,1\,8\,¢ \\ \hline \end{array}$$

Container	Estimate	Actual
A		
B		
C		
D		
E		
F		
G		

Picture for container _____

$$
\begin{array}{r} 4 \\ -\ 3 \\ \hline \end{array}
\qquad
\begin{array}{r} 11 \\ -\ 2 \\ \hline \end{array}
\qquad
\begin{array}{r} 8 \\ -\ 7 \\ \hline \end{array}
\qquad
\begin{array}{r} 16 \\ -\ 7 \\ \hline \end{array}
\qquad
\begin{array}{r} 6 \\ -\ 4 \\ \hline \end{array}
$$

$$
\begin{array}{r} 10 \\ -\ 8 \\ \hline \end{array}
\qquad
\begin{array}{r} 8 \\ -\ 6 \\ \hline \end{array}
\qquad
\begin{array}{r} 6 \\ -\ 5 \\ \hline \end{array}
\qquad
\begin{array}{r} 12 \\ -\ 3 \\ \hline \end{array}
\qquad
\begin{array}{r} 5 \\ -\ 4 \\ \hline \end{array}
$$

$$
\begin{array}{r} 13 \\ -\ 4 \\ \hline \end{array}
\qquad
\begin{array}{r} 7 \\ -\ 6 \\ \hline \end{array}
\qquad
\begin{array}{r} 5 \\ -\ 3 \\ \hline \end{array}
\qquad
\begin{array}{r} 9 \\ -\ 8 \\ \hline \end{array}
\qquad
\begin{array}{r} 15 \\ -\ 6 \\ \hline \end{array}
$$

$$
\begin{array}{r} 7 \\ -\ 5 \\ \hline \end{array}
\qquad
\begin{array}{r} 11 \\ -\ 2 \\ \hline \end{array}
\qquad
\begin{array}{r} 14 \\ -\ 5 \\ \hline \end{array}
\qquad
\begin{array}{r} 9 \\ -\ 7 \\ \hline \end{array}
\qquad
\begin{array}{r} 17 \\ -\ 8 \\ \hline \end{array}
$$

$$
\begin{array}{r} 8 \\ -\ 6 \\ \hline \end{array}
\qquad
\begin{array}{r} 5 \\ -\ 4 \\ \hline \end{array}
\qquad
\begin{array}{r} 16 \\ -\ 7 \\ \hline \end{array}
\qquad
\begin{array}{r} 7 \\ -\ 6 \\ \hline \end{array}
\qquad
\begin{array}{r} 10 \\ -\ 1 \\ \hline \end{array}
$$

Score: _____

Name ●
(Draw a 3-inch line segment.)

Date ●
(Draw a $3\frac{1}{2}$-inch line segment.)

1. There were 43 pennies in the penny jar. Mrs. Kaplan put 17 more pennies in the jar. How many pennies are in the jar now?

   Number sentence _____ Answer _____

2. Draw a picture to show 504. (Use ☐ for 100, ☐ for 10, ☐ for 1.)

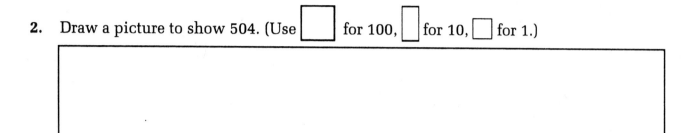

3. Color the thermometer to show 54°F.

4. It's afternoon. What time is it? _____

5. Divide each shape into fourths.

Shade $\frac{3}{4}$.

Shade $\frac{2}{4}$.

Shade $\frac{1}{4}$.

6. Write the examples vertically. Find the answers.

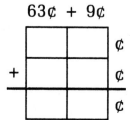
63¢ + 9¢

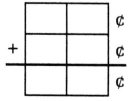
27¢ + 53¢

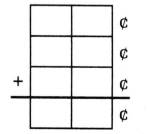
54¢ + 12¢ + 24¢

Name _____

Date _____

1. There were 16 dimes in the dime jar. Mrs. McDonough put 34 more dimes in the jar. How many dimes are in the jar now?

    Number sentence _____   Answer _____

2. Draw a picture to show 350. (Use ⬜ for 100, ▯ for 10, ▢ for 1.)

3. Color the thermometer to show 38°F.

4. It's morning. What time is it? _____

5. Divide each shape into fourths.

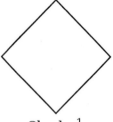      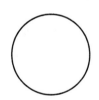

    Shade $\frac{1}{4}$.   Shade $\frac{2}{4}$.   Shade $\frac{3}{4}$.

6. Write the examples vertically. Find the answers.

    54¢ + 16¢   63¢ + 24¢   19¢ + 14¢ + 51¢

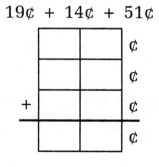

10	10	10	10	10
− 8	− 4	− 1	− 7	− 3

10	10	10	10	10
− 5	− 2	− 9	− 6	− 0

10	10	10	10	10
− 10	− 5	− 9	− 6	− 2

10	10	10	10	10
− 3	− 7	− 1	− 4	− 8

10	10	10	10	10
− 10	− 0	− 6	− 4	− 8

Score: _____

Name ●————————————————————————————●

(Measure this line segment using inches. _____ ")

Date ●

(Draw a $2\frac{1}{2}$" line segment.)

1. Forty-seven children voted no and thirty-nine children voted yes. How many children voted?

Number sentence _____ Answer _____

2. One of these numbers is my secret number. Cross out the numbers that cannot be my secret number.

It is not an odd number.
It has only one digit.
It is greater than 7.

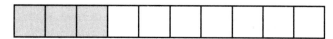

5   6   7   8   9   10   11   12   13   14

What is my secret number? _____

3. Write the fraction that tells how much is shaded. _____

Write the fraction that tells how much is not shaded. _____

4. Show 7:55 on the clockface.

5. Find the answers.

$$\begin{array}{r} 10 \\ -\ 4 \\ \hline \end{array} \qquad \begin{array}{r} 10 \\ -\ 7 \\ \hline \end{array} \qquad \begin{array}{r} 10 \\ -\ 2 \\ \hline \end{array} \qquad \begin{array}{r} 10 \\ -\ 9 \\ \hline \end{array} \qquad \begin{array}{r} 10 \\ -\ 5 \\ \hline \end{array}$$

6. Find the answers.

$$\begin{array}{r} 2\ 9¢ \\ 3\ 1¢ \\ +\ 2\ 4¢ \\ \hline \end{array} \qquad 58¢ + 23¢ \qquad 5 + 8 + 4 + 3 + 2 + 7 = \text{_____}$$

Name _____   **LESSON 87B**

Date _____   **Math 2**

1. Fifty-three children in grade 2 walk to school. Thirty-seven grade 2 children ride to school. How many children are in grade 2?

    Number sentence _____   Answer _____

2. One of these numbers is my sister's secret number. Cross out the numbers that cannot be my sister's secret number.

    It is not an even number.
    It has two digits.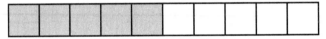
    It is less than 12.

    | 5 6 7 8 9 10 11 12 13 14 |

    What is my sister's secret number? _____

3. Write the fraction that tells how much is shaded. _____

    Write the fraction that tells how much is not shaded. _____

4. Show 8:25 on the clockface.

5. Find the answers.

10	10	10	10	10
− 6	− 3	− 8	− 1	− 5

6. Find the answers.

    3 2¢   24¢ + 57¢   7 + 4 + 2 + 7 + 6 + 3 = _____
    1 4¢
    + 2 7¢
    _____

Name _____

Before 1965 1965-1969 1970-1974 1975-1979 1980-1984 1985-1989 1990-now

20							
18							
16							
14							
12							
10							
8							
6							
4							
2							
0							

Before 1965 1965-1969 1970-1974 1975-1979 1980-1984 1985-1989 1990-now

How many pennies were minted in the years 1980 through 1984? _____

How many pennies were minted in the years 1985 through 1989? _____

When were most of your pennies minted? _____

10 − 8	10 − 4	10 − 1	10 − 7	10 − 3
10 − 5	10 − 2	10 − 9	10 − 6	10 − 0
10 − 10	10 − 5	10 − 9	10 − 6	10 − 2
10 − 3	10 − 7	10 − 1	10 − 4	10 − 8
10 − 10	10 − 0	10 − 6	10 − 4	10 − 8

Score: _____

Name •———————————————————•
(Measure this line segment using inches. _____")

Date •
(Draw a $1\frac{1}{2}$" line segment.)

1. There are 83 children in grade 2 at Haley School. Ten second graders were absent on Monday. How many grade 2 children were in school?

Number sentence _____ Answer _____

2. Shelly has a half dozen dimes and a dozen pennies.

How many dimes is this? _____   How much money is that? _____

How many pennies is this? _____   How much money is that? _____

How much money does Shelly have? _____

3. This is a tally to show how many children chose each color.

yellow	ЖЖ ЖЖ
purple	ЖЖ ||
pink	ЖЖ

Shade the graph to show the colors the children chose.

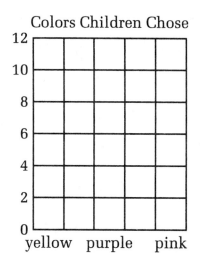

Colors Children Chose

4. It's morning.
What time is it?

_____

It's evening.
What time is it?

_____

5. Find the answers.

$$\begin{array}{r} 2\ 6\ \cancel{c} \\ +\ 4\ 6\ \cancel{c} \\ \hline \end{array}$$

$$\begin{array}{r} 3\ 7\ \cancel{c} \\ +\ 4\ 2\ \cancel{c} \\ \hline \end{array}$$

$$\begin{array}{r} 1\ 6\ \cancel{c} \\ 4\ 3\ \cancel{c} \\ +\ 2\ 8\ \cancel{c} \\ \hline \end{array}$$

Name _____   **LESSON 88B**

Date _____   *Math 2*

1. The label on the bag says that there are 72 pieces of candy in the bag. Mindy ate 10 pieces. How many pieces are left?

   Number sentence _____ Answer _____

2. Curtis has nine dimes and a half dozen pennies.

   How many dimes is this? _____   How much money is that? _____

   How many pennies is this? _____   How much money is that? _____

   How much money does Curtis have? _____

3. This is a tally to show how many children chose each color.

red	卌 |||
blue	卌 卌	
green	|||

   Shade the graph to show the colors the children chose.

   Colors Children Chose

	red	blue	green
12			
10			
8			
6			
4			
2			
0			

4. It's morning. What time is it?

   _____

   It's evening. What time is it?

   _____

5. Find the answers.

   $$\begin{array}{r} 2\ 7\ ¢ \\ +\ 5\ 3\ ¢ \\ \hline \end{array}$$
   $$\begin{array}{r} 1\ 6\ ¢ \\ +\ 5\ 1\ ¢ \\ \hline \end{array}$$
   $$\begin{array}{r} 1\ 3\ ¢ \\ 3\ 8\ ¢ \\ +\ 3\ 7\ ¢ \\ \hline \end{array}$$

8 × 10	10 × 4	7 × 10	5 × 10	10 × 2
6 × 10	10 × 1	10 × 3	9 × 10	10 × 6
10 × 10	10 × 5	2 × 10	10 × 8	6 × 10
3 × 10	10 × 7	0 × 10	6 × 10	10 × 9
8 × 10	10 × 2	4 × 10	10 × 0	7 × 10

Score: _____

Name _____ •

(Draw a $4\frac{1}{2}$" line segment.)

Date _____ •————————————————•

(Measure this line segment using inches. _____")

1. Blake bought a marker for 48¢ and an eraser for 37¢. How much money did he spend?

Number sentence _____ Answer _____

2. Write these examples using the multiplication symbol.

5 groups of 10   3 groups of 10   9 groups of 10

_____   _____   _____

3. Draw a picture to show 2 hundreds + 3 ones.

What number does the picture show? _____

4. Use the graph to answer the questions.

How many children like hiking? _____

How many children like skating? _____

How many children like only hiking? _____

What does Curt like? _____

Sports Children Like
Hiking   Skating
Phil
May   Bob   Jill
Leah   Curt   Skip
Sarah

5. Shade the thermometer to show 74°F.

100°F
90°F
80°F
70°F
60°F
50°F
40°F
30°F
20°F
10°F
0°F
−10°F
−20°F

6. Find each product.

$3 \times 10 =$ _____ $8 \times 10 =$ _____ $6 \times 10 =$ _____ $0 \times 10 =$ _____

7. How much money is this? _____

2-89Wa

Name _____

Date _____

1. Alexis bought a note pad for 64¢ and a pencil for 19¢. How much money did she spend?

   Number sentence _____ Answer _____

2. Write these examples using the multiplication symbol.

   4 groups of 10   8 groups of 10   2 groups of 10

   _____   _____   _____

3. Draw a picture to show 3 hundreds + 2 tens + 7 ones.

   +---+
   | |
   | |
   | |
   +---+

   What number does the picture show? _____

4. Use the graph to answer the questions.

   How many children like soccer? _____

   How many children like swimming? _____

   How many children like only soccer? _____

   What does Anna like? _____

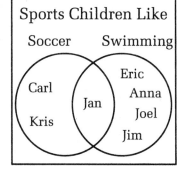

Sports Children Like

Soccer   Swimming

Carl   Jan   Eric
Kris   Anna
               Joel
               Jim

5. Shade the thermometer to show 48°F.

100°F
90°F
80°F
70°F
60°F
50°F
40°F
30°F
20°F
10°F
0°F
−10°F
−20°F

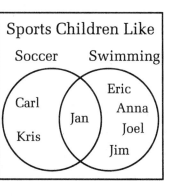

6. Find each product.

   2 × 10 = _____   7 × 10 = _____   9 × 10 = _____   1 × 10 = _____

7. How much money is this? _____

2-89Wb

Name _____

Date _____

1. Amanda bought a ruler for 27¢ and an eraser for 46¢. How much money did she spend?

   Number sentence _____ Answer _____

2. One of these names is the name of my dog. Cross out the names that cannot be my dog's name.

   It is not the name that is last. | Lady | Duffer | Rover | Spot | Ebony |
   It does not have 4 letters.
   It is not the name in the middle.

   What is my dog's name? _____

3. What temperature does the thermometer show? _____°F

4. Write fractions that tell how much is shaded.

    _____   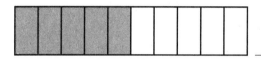 _____

5. Measure the line segment using inches. _____ inches

   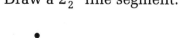

   Draw a $2\frac{1}{2}$" line segment.

   •

6. Find the answers.

   $\begin{array}{r} 5\ 6\ ¢ \\ +\ 3\ 2\ ¢ \\ \hline \end{array}$ $\begin{array}{r} 6\ 8\ ¢ \\ +\ 1\ 7\ ¢ \\ \hline \end{array}$ $\begin{array}{r} 2\ 4\ ¢ \\ +\ 3\ 6\ ¢ \\ \hline \end{array}$ 42¢ + 19¢

   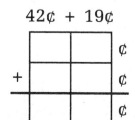

2-90Aa

(Optional: Use if tangram sets are not available.)

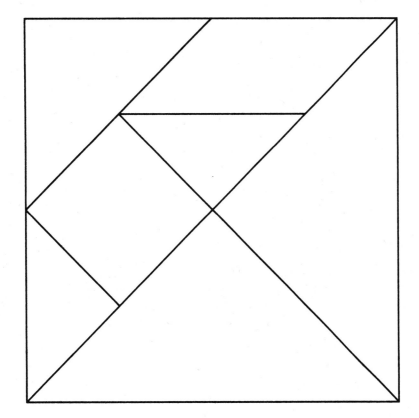

Cover the shapes using only one set of tangram pieces.

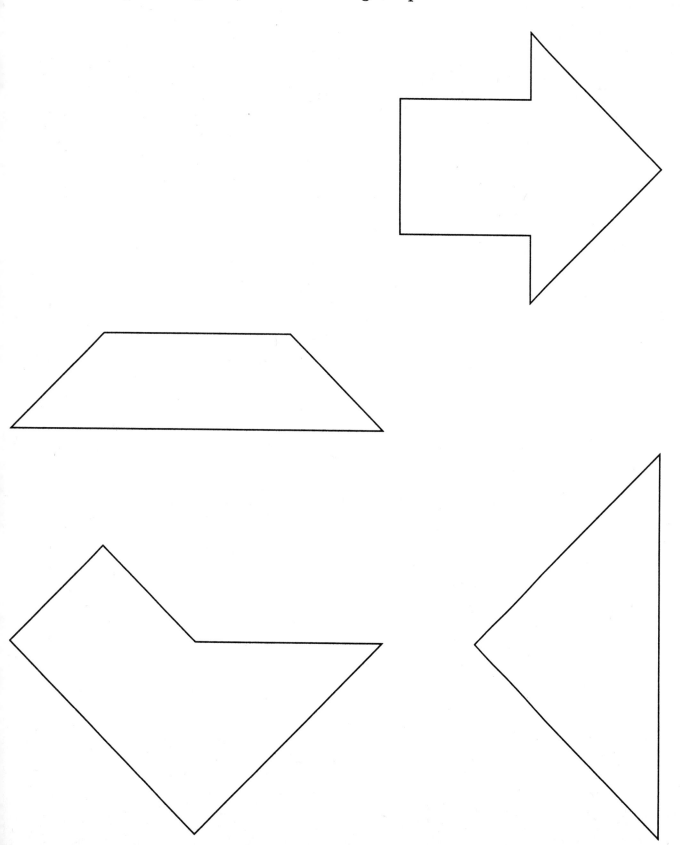

Cover this shape using only the triangles.

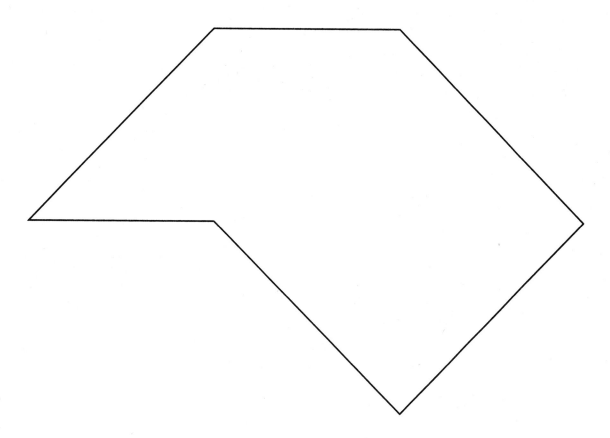

Cover this shape using only the square, the parallelogram, and two small triangles.

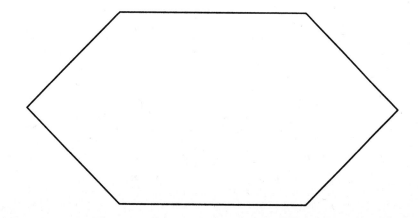

10 − 8	10 − 4	10 − 1	10 − 7	10 − 3
10 − 5	10 − 2	10 − 9	10 − 6	10 − 0
10 − 10	10 − 5	10 − 9	10 − 6	10 − 2
10 − 3	10 − 7	10 − 1	10 − 4	10 − 8
10 − 10	10 − 0	10 − 6	10 − 4	10 − 8

Score: _____

Name _____

8 $\times\ 10$	10 $\times\ 4$	7 $\times\ 10$	5 $\times\ 10$	10 $\times\ 2$
6 $\times\ 10$	10 $\times\ 1$	10 $\times\ 3$	9 $\times\ 10$	10 $\times\ 6$
10 $\times\ 10$	10 $\times\ 5$	2 $\times\ 10$	10 $\times\ 8$	6 $\times\ 10$
3 $\times\ 10$	10 $\times\ 7$	0 $\times\ 10$	6 $\times\ 10$	10 $\times\ 9$
8 $\times\ 10$	10 $\times\ 2$	4 $\times\ 10$	10 $\times\ 0$	7 $\times\ 10$

Score: _____

Name •
(Draw a 4" line segment.)

Date •
(Draw a $2\frac{1}{2}$" line segment.)

1. Marsha counted the tiles and put them in groups of 10. When she finished, she counted 3 groups of tiles. Draw a picture to show the tiles.

```



```

Marsha has _____ groups of _____ tiles.

How many tiles does she have? _____

2. Circle the largest and the smallest numbers.

| 71 | 47 | 24 | 38 |

Find their sum. _____

Find the sum of the two numbers that are not circled. _____

3. Write 437 in expanded form. _____

Write the number for 200 + 60 + 7. _____

Write the number for 300 + 8. _____

4. Find the answers.

10 less than 61 = _____   10 − 7 = _____   10 − 4 = _____

13 − 9 = _____   7 × 10 = _____   4 × 10 = _____

5. Color the shapes that are congruent to the oval on the left.

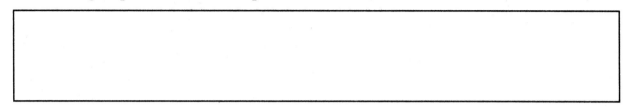

1. Stephen counted the cubes and put them in groups of 10. When he finished, he counted 5 groups of cubes. Draw a picture to show the cubes.

   Stephen has _____ groups of _____ cubes.

   How many cubes does he have? _____

2. Circle the largest and the smallest numbers.

   | 37 | 26 | 54 | 47 |

   Find their sum. _____

   Find the sum of the two numbers that are not circled. _____

3. Write 163 in expanded form. _____

   Write the number for 300 + 20 + 9. _____

   Write the number for 400 + 70. _____

4. Find the answers.

   1 less than 40 = _____   10 − 6 = _____   10 − 3 = _____

   12 − 9 = _____   5 × 10 = _____   3 × 10 = _____

5. Color the shapes that are congruent to the rectangle on the left.

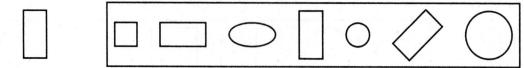

11 − 6	15 − 7	7 − 4	13 − 6	9 − 5
17 − 9	13 − 7	15 − 8	7 − 3	11 − 5
9 − 4	17 − 8	7 − 4	11 − 6	13 − 6
15 − 7	9 − 5	7 − 3	15 − 8	11 − 5
13 − 7	17 − 9	9 − 4	11 − 6	17 − 8

Score: _____

2-92Fa

Name •
(Draw a 4" line segment.)

Date •
(Draw a line segment that is one inch shorter than the line segment for your name.)

1. Amber has 5 dimes and 8 pennies. Eileen has 6 pennies and 3 dimes. How much money does each girl have?

   Amber _____   Eileen _____

   How much money do they have altogether?

   Number sentence _____   Answer _____

2. Write 437 in expanded form. _____

   Write the number for 200 + 60 + 7. _____

3. Shade the bar graph to show how many children are in each grade at Adams Elementary School.

   Grade 1   40 children

   Grade 2   60 children

   Grade 3   50 children

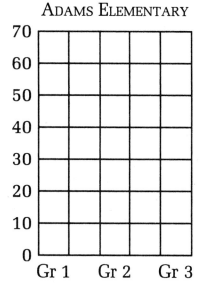

ADAMS ELEMENTARY

4. Write the fraction that tells how much is shaded. _____

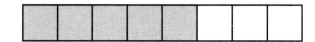

   Write the fraction that tells how much is not shaded. _____

5. Find the answers.

   10 − 4 = _____   4 × 10 = _____

   51 − 10 = _____   0 × 10 = _____

   ```
      5 ¢          1 2 ¢
     4 7 ¢         4 9 ¢
   + 2 3 ¢       + 2 9 ¢
   ```

Name _____

Date _____

1. Evonne has 7 pennies and 4 dimes. Joann has 3 dimes and 9 pennies. How much money does each girl have?

   Evonne _____   Joann _____

   How much money do they have altogether?

   Number sentence _____   Answer _____

2. Write 420 in expanded form. _____

   Write the number for 6 + 300 + 40. _____

3. Shade the bar graph to show how many children are in each grade at Rock Canyon Elementary School.

   Grade 1   20 children

   Grade 2   40 children

   Grade 3   50 children

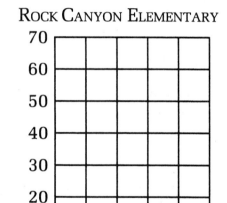

ROCK CANYON ELEMENTARY

4. Write the fraction that tells how much is shaded. _____

   Write the fraction that tells how much is not shaded. _____

5. Find the answers.

   10 − 7 = _____   8 × 10 = _____

   63 − 10 = _____   1 × 10 = _____

$$\begin{array}{r} 1\,7\,¢ \\ 6\,¢ \\ +\,5\,4\,¢ \\ \hline \end{array}$$
$$\begin{array}{r} 2\,8\,¢ \\ 1\,4\,¢ \\ +\,3\,8\,¢ \\ \hline \end{array}$$

$$\begin{array}{r} 11 \\ -\ 6 \\ \hline \end{array} \qquad \begin{array}{r} 15 \\ -\ 7 \\ \hline \end{array} \qquad \begin{array}{r} 7 \\ -\ 4 \\ \hline \end{array} \qquad \begin{array}{r} 13 \\ -\ 6 \\ \hline \end{array} \qquad \begin{array}{r} 9 \\ -\ 5 \\ \hline \end{array}$$

$$\begin{array}{r} 17 \\ -\ 9 \\ \hline \end{array} \qquad \begin{array}{r} 13 \\ -\ 7 \\ \hline \end{array} \qquad \begin{array}{r} 15 \\ -\ 8 \\ \hline \end{array} \qquad \begin{array}{r} 7 \\ -\ 3 \\ \hline \end{array} \qquad \begin{array}{r} 11 \\ -\ 5 \\ \hline \end{array}$$

$$\begin{array}{r} 9 \\ -\ 4 \\ \hline \end{array} \qquad \begin{array}{r} 17 \\ -\ 8 \\ \hline \end{array} \qquad \begin{array}{r} 7 \\ -\ 4 \\ \hline \end{array} \qquad \begin{array}{r} 11 \\ -\ 6 \\ \hline \end{array} \qquad \begin{array}{r} 13 \\ -\ 6 \\ \hline \end{array}$$

$$\begin{array}{r} 15 \\ -\ 7 \\ \hline \end{array} \qquad \begin{array}{r} 9 \\ -\ 5 \\ \hline \end{array} \qquad \begin{array}{r} 7 \\ -\ 3 \\ \hline \end{array} \qquad \begin{array}{r} 15 \\ -\ 8 \\ \hline \end{array} \qquad \begin{array}{r} 11 \\ -\ 5 \\ \hline \end{array}$$

$$\begin{array}{r} 13 \\ -\ 7 \\ \hline \end{array} \qquad \begin{array}{r} 17 \\ -\ 9 \\ \hline \end{array} \qquad \begin{array}{r} 9 \\ -\ 4 \\ \hline \end{array} \qquad \begin{array}{r} 11 \\ -\ 6 \\ \hline \end{array} \qquad \begin{array}{r} 17 \\ -\ 8 \\ \hline \end{array}$$

Score: _____

Name ●
(Draw a 3" line segment.)

Date ●

(Draw a line segment 2" longer than the line segment for your name.)

1. Sixteen children in Room 14 at Savin Rock Elementary School wrote pen pal letters. They sent nine of the letters to children in Room 10 at Grandview Elementary School. How many letters do they have left to send?

    Number sentence _____ Answer _____

2. How much money is this? Write the amount two ways. _____ _____

3. Show 2:35 on the clockface.

4. Divide this square in fourths using only horizontal line segments.

    Shade $\frac{1}{4}$.

    Divide this square in fourths using only vertical line segments.

    Shade $\frac{2}{4}$.

    Divide this square in fourths using only oblique line segments.

    Shade $\frac{3}{4}$.

5. Find the answers.

    10 less than 54 = _____   10 more than 31 = _____   63¢ + 18¢ = _____

    8 + 3 + 9 + 2 + 6 + 1 + 7 + 4 = _____

Name _____

Date _____

1. Mrs. Roy bought eighteen oranges on March 5th. During the next four days the children ate ten oranges. How many oranges are left?

   Number sentence _____ Answer _____

2. How much money is this? Write the amount in two ways. _____ _____

3. Show 4:50 on the clockface.

4. Divide this rectangle in fourths using only horizontal line segments.

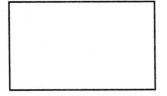

   Shade $\frac{2}{4}$.

   Divide this rectangle in fourths using only vertical line segments.

   Shade $\frac{3}{4}$.

   Divide this rectangle in fourths using a vertical and a horizontal line segment.

   Shade $\frac{1}{4}$.

5. Find the answers.

   10 more than 63 = _____   10 less than 41 = _____   47¢ + 23¢ = _____

   6 + 7 + 3 + 2 + 4 + 5 + 1 = _____

$$
\begin{array}{r} 5 \\ -\ 1 \\ \hline \end{array}
\qquad
\begin{array}{r} 10 \\ -\ 6 \\ \hline \end{array}
\qquad
\begin{array}{r} 14 \\ -\ 9 \\ \hline \end{array}
\qquad
\begin{array}{r} 7 \\ -\ 6 \\ \hline \end{array}
\qquad
\begin{array}{r} 5 \\ -\ 3 \\ \hline \end{array}
$$

$$
\begin{array}{r} 13 \\ -\ 4 \\ \hline \end{array}
\qquad
\begin{array}{r} 9 \\ -\ 2 \\ \hline \end{array}
\qquad
\begin{array}{r} 8 \\ -\ 6 \\ \hline \end{array}
\qquad
\begin{array}{r} 10 \\ -\ 3 \\ \hline \end{array}
\qquad
\begin{array}{r} 16 \\ -\ 7 \\ \hline \end{array}
$$

$$
\begin{array}{r} 6 \\ -\ 3 \\ \hline \end{array}
\qquad
\begin{array}{r} 10 \\ -\ 2 \\ \hline \end{array}
\qquad
\begin{array}{r} 15 \\ -\ 9 \\ \hline \end{array}
\qquad
\begin{array}{r} 8 \\ -\ 7 \\ \hline \end{array}
\qquad
\begin{array}{r} 10 \\ -\ 7 \\ \hline \end{array}
$$

$$
\begin{array}{r} 4 \\ -\ 3 \\ \hline \end{array}
\qquad
\begin{array}{r} 17 \\ -\ 8 \\ \hline \end{array}
\qquad
\begin{array}{r} 10 \\ -\ 4 \\ \hline \end{array}
\qquad
\begin{array}{r} 7 \\ -\ 0 \\ \hline \end{array}
\qquad
\begin{array}{r} 9 \\ -\ 7 \\ \hline \end{array}
$$

$$
\begin{array}{r} 18 \\ -\ 9 \\ \hline \end{array}
\qquad
\begin{array}{r} 6 \\ -\ 5 \\ \hline \end{array}
\qquad
\begin{array}{r} 8 \\ -\ 2 \\ \hline \end{array}
\qquad
\begin{array}{r} 10 \\ -\ 8 \\ \hline \end{array}
\qquad
\begin{array}{r} 12 \\ -\ 3 \\ \hline \end{array}
$$

Score: _____

Name _____•
(Measure this line segment. _____")

Date •_____•
(Measure this line segment. _____")

1. Mary bought a package of candy. There are 10 candies in a package. Mary ate 6 candies. How many candies are left?

   Number sentence _____ Answer _____

2. Put these numbers in order from least to greatest.

   | 29   43   27   48   19 |

   ____ ____ ____ ____ ____
   least   greatest

   Add the least and the greatest numbers. _____

   Add the other three numbers. _____

3. About how tall is your teacher? _____

4. Brian has 3 dimes and 16 pennies. How much money is this?

   Write the amount two ways. _____   _____

5. My favorite time of day is 8:40 p.m.
   Show that time on the clock.

   Is it morning or evening? _____

6. Write the fact family number sentences for 2, 7, and 9.

   _____   _____

   _____   _____

Name _____

Date _____

1. Silvia bought a package of pencils. There are 10 pencils in a package. Silvia gave 4 pencils to her sister. How many pencils does she have left?

   Number sentence _____ Answer _____

2. Put these numbers in order from least to greatest.

   | 38 24 33 18 26 | ____ ____ ____ ____ ____

   least   greatest

   Add the least and the greatest numbers. _____

   Add the other three numbers. _____

3. About how long is your bed? _____

4. Evan has 5 dimes and 14 pennies. How much money is this?

   Write the amount two ways. _____   _____

5. What is your favorite time of day?

   _____

   Show that time on the clock.

6. Write the fact family number sentences for 1, 8, and 9.

   _____   _____

   _____   _____

Name _____

Date _____

1. James has 3 dimes and 7 pennies. George has 8 pennies and 4 dimes. How much money does each boy have?

James _____   George _____

How much money do they have altogether?

Number sentence _____   Answer _____

2. Write these numbers in order from least to greatest.

| 142 316 221 164 79 |

_____   _____   _____   _____   _____

least   greatest

3. What number does this picture show? _____

| 100 | 100 | 100 | 10 | 1 | 1 | 1 | 1 | 1 |

4. Show 6:20 on the clockface.

5. Write the fact family number sentences for 3, 7, and 10.

_____   _____

_____   _____

6. Find the answers.

$37¢ + 43¢$ $28¢ + 31¢$ $\begin{array}{r} 4\,6\,¢ \\ +\ 2\,5\,¢ \\ \hline \end{array}$

11 − 6	15 − 7	7 − 4	13 − 6	9 − 5
17 − 9	13 − 7	15 − 8	7 − 3	11 − 5
9 − 4	17 − 8	7 − 4	11 − 6	13 − 6
15 − 7	9 − 5	7 − 3	15 − 8	11 − 5
13 − 7	17 − 9	9 − 4	11 − 6	17 − 8

Score: _____

Name ●
(Draw a 4" line segment.)

Date ●
(Draw a $1\frac{1}{2}$" line segment.)

1. Justin has 2 one-dollar bills, 3 dimes, and 7 pennies. How much money does he have?

    Answer _____

2. Use the graph to answer the questions.

    CHILDREN'S FAVORITE SPORT

    How many children chose skating? _____

    How many more children chose biking than chose skiing? _____

    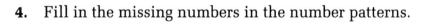

3. Shade the thermometer to show 42°F.

4. Fill in the missing numbers in the number patterns.

    ____ , ____ , ____ , ____ , ____ , ____ , 24, 26, 28

    ____ , ____ , ____ , 50, 45, 40, ____ , ____ , ____

5. Draw a line of symmetry in each shape.

    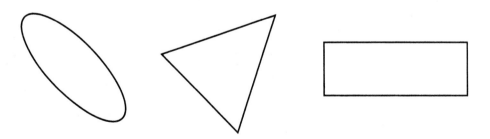

6. Find the sums.

    79¢ + 36¢   43¢ + 82¢   76¢ + 94¢

1. Nadine has 3 one-dollar bills, 5 dimes, and 1 penny. How much money does she have?

   Answer _____

2. Use the graph to answer the questions.

CHILDREN'S FAVORITE SPORT					
swimming					
soccer					
baseball					

   0 2 4 6 8 10

   How many children chose soccer? _____

   How many more children chose swimming than chose baseball? _____

3. Shade the thermometer to show 18°F.

4. Fill in the missing numbers in the number patterns.

   _____ , _____ , _____ , _____ , _____ , _____ , 25, 27, 29

   _____ , _____ , _____ , 35, 40, 45, _____ , _____ , _____

5. Draw a line of symmetry in each shape.

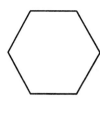
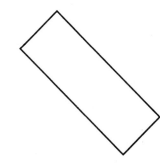

6. Find the sums.

   48¢ + 91¢   63¢ + 57¢   87¢ + 84¢

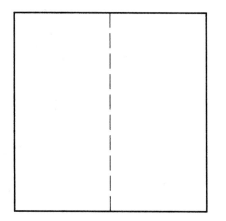

one half of _____ is _____

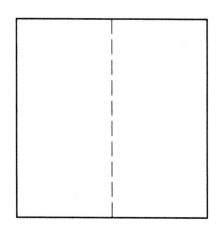

one half of _____ is _____

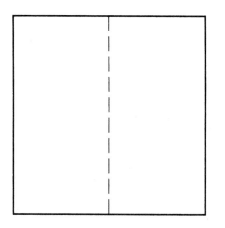

one half of _____ is _____

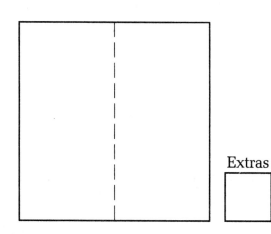

Extras

one half of _____ is _____

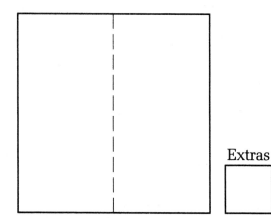

Extras

one half of _____ is _____

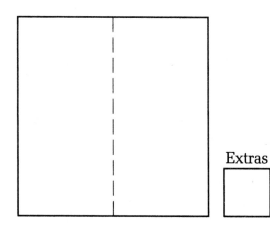

Extras

one half of _____ is _____

9 + 1	2 + 2	6 + 4	5 + 1	0 + 7	9 + 9	7 + 3	1 + 6	2 + 5	5 + 4
9 + 4	2 + 0	8 + 7	4 + 1	6 + 6	7 + 8	3 + 2	9 + 8	0 + 8	4 + 6
5 + 2	3 + 9	0 + 6	8 + 1	3 + 3	7 + 4	7 + 0	1 + 5	6 + 7	2 + 3
1 + 0	5 + 5	7 + 6	3 + 4	2 + 6	9 + 5	7 + 2	4 + 9	0 + 3	6 + 8
8 + 2	3 + 5	1 + 7	0 + 0	6 + 2	5 + 7	1 + 4	8 + 6	2 + 9	5 + 0
6 + 3	0 + 5	3 + 7	4 + 4	9 + 2	1 + 8	6 + 5	2 + 4	8 + 8	0 + 9
4 + 2	7 + 7	9 + 0	9 + 6	5 + 8	0 + 1	3 + 6	7 + 9	6 + 0	4 + 8
7 + 1	2 + 6	4 + 7	1 + 2	4 + 5	8 + 9	3 + 0	8 + 3	1 + 9	5 + 6
1 + 1	3 + 8	0 + 2	5 + 9	9 + 3	2 + 7	8 + 0	4 + 3	6 + 9	1 + 3
8 + 5	4 + 0	5 + 3	2 + 8	3 + 1	7 + 5	9 + 7	0 + 4	8 + 4	6 + 1

Name ●

(Draw a 4½" line segment.)

Date ●

(Draw a 3" line segment.)

1. The kindergarten children made a graph to show the shoes and sneakers they were wearing. They counted 10 shoes and 14 sneakers. Draw a picture to show the shoes and sneakers. Circle the pairs.

How many children are in the kindergarten class? _____

2. What number does this picture show? _____

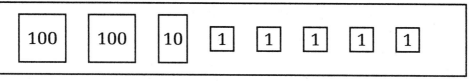

Write the number in expanded form. _____

3. I have 3 dimes, 4 nickels, and 6 pennies. Draw the coins. How much money is this? Write the amount two ways.

_____   _____

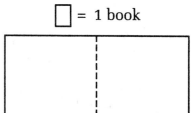

$\square$ = 1 book

4. Show how two children will share ten books equally.

How many books will each child have? _____

one half of 10 is _____

5. I can see the stars. What time is it?

Answer _____

1. The first grade children made a graph to show the shoes and sneakers they were wearing. They counted 8 shoes and 12 sneakers. Draw a picture to show the shoes and sneakers. Circle the pairs.

   How many children are in the first grade class? _____

2. What number does this picture show? _____

   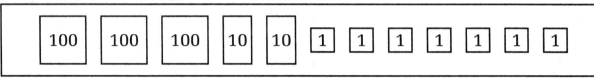

   Write the number in expanded form. _____

3. I have 4 dimes, 3 nickels, and 6 pennies. Draw the coins. How much money is this? Write the amount two ways.

   _____   _____

4. Show how two children will share six books equally.

   How many books will each child have? _____

   □ = 1 book

5. The sun is shining. What time is it?

   Answer _____

   one half of 6 is _____

11 − 6	15 − 7	7 − 4	13 − 6	9 − 5
17 − 9	13 − 7	15 − 8	7 − 3	11 − 5
9 − 4	17 − 8	7 − 4	11 − 6	13 − 6
15 − 7	9 − 5	7 − 3	15 − 8	11 − 5
13 − 7	17 − 9	9 − 4	11 − 6	17 − 8

Score: _____

Name •

(Draw a 3½" line segment.)

Date •

(Draw a 3" line segment.)

1. There are 27 children in Room 6, 22 children in Room 7, and 25 children in Room 8. How many children are in the three classes?

   Number sentence _____ Answer _____

2. Twelve children chose vanilla ice cream, nine children chose chocolate ice cream, and five children chose strawberry ice cream.

   Shade the graph to show the ice cream flavors the children chose.

   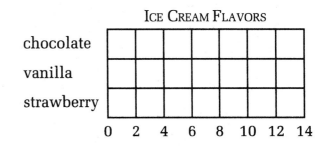

   ICE CREAM FLAVORS

   chocolate

   vanilla

   strawberry

   0 2 4 6 8 10 12 14

   How many more children chose vanilla than chose chocolate? _____

3. Write 806 in expanded form. _____

   Draw a picture to show this amount. (Use ▭ for 100, ▯ for 10, ▢ for 1.)

4. Show how 2 children will share 11 pennies equally.

   How many pennies will each child have? _____

   How many extra pennies are there? _____

   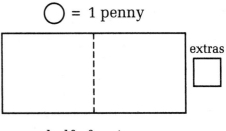

   ○ = 1 penny

   extras

   one half of 11 is _____

5. Find the answers.

   $7 \times 10 =$ _____ $4 \times 10 =$ _____ $41 - 10 =$ _____

   $8 + 6 + 5 + 2 + 3 + 5 + 3 + 4 + 5 + 1 + 2 =$ _____

1. There are 18 children in Room 9, 23 children in Room 10, and 25 children in Room 11. How many children are in the three classes?

   Number sentence _____ Answer _____

2. Seven children chose a banana, ten children chose an apple, and eleven children chose an orange.

   Shade the graph to show the fruits the children chose.

   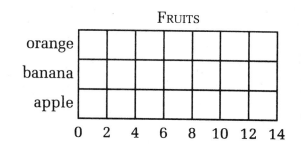

   How many more children chose an orange than chose an apple? _____

3. Write 350 in expanded form. _____

   Draw a picture to show this amount. (Use ☐ for 100, ☐ for 10, ☐ for 1.)

4. Show how 2 children will share 9 pennies equally.

   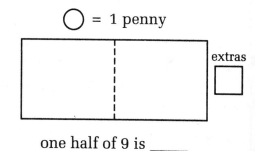

   How many pennies will each child have? _____

   How many extra pennies are there? _____

   one half of 9 is _____

5. Find the answers.

   $3 \times 10 =$ _____ $6 \times 10 =$ _____ $24 - 10 =$ _____

   $4 + 5 + 2 + 3 + 7 + 9 + 5 + 1 + 1 + 4 =$ _____

5 − 1	10 − 6	14 − 9	7 − 6	5 − 3
13 − 4	9 − 2	8 − 6	10 − 3	16 − 7
6 − 3	10 − 2	15 − 9	8 − 7	10 − 7
4 − 3	17 − 8	10 − 4	7 − 0	9 − 7
18 − 9	6 − 5	8 − 2	10 − 8	12 − 3

Score: _____

(Draw a line segment 1" shorter than the date line segment.)

1. Ellen has 5 dimes and 8 pennies. Kay has 2 dimes and 14 pennies. How much money does each girl have?

   Ellen _____   Kay _____   Who has the most money? _____

   Write a number sentence to show how to find how much money the girls have altogether.

   Number sentence _____ Answer _____

   Show two ways to write how much money they have altogether. _____ _____

2. Show how the children will share the markers equally.

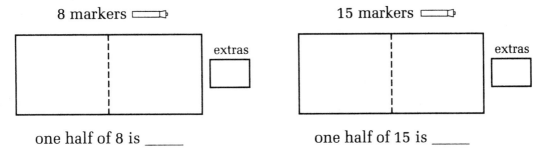

   8 markers ▭➤   15 markers ▭➤

   one half of 8 is _____   one half of 15 is _____

3. Two fact family number sentences are 6 + 7 = 13 and 13 − 6 = 7. Write the other two fact family number sentences.

   _____   _____

4. How much money is this? _____

5. Find the answers.

   $$\begin{array}{r} 1\,6\,¢ \\ 2\,5\,¢ \\ +\,3\,9\,¢ \\ \hline \end{array}$$ $$\begin{array}{r} 4\,9\,¢ \\ +\,3\,3\,¢ \\ \hline \end{array}$$

   5 × 10 = _____   10 − 8 = _____

   15 − 7 = _____   17 − 9 = _____

1. Andrew has 2 dimes and 17 pennies. Danny has 3 dimes and 5 pennies. How much money does each boy have?

   Andrew _____   Danny _____   Who has the most money? _____
   Write a number sentence to show how to find how much money the boys have altogether.

   Number sentence _____ Answer _____

   Show two ways to write how much money they have altogether. _____ _____

2. Show how the children will share the markers equally.

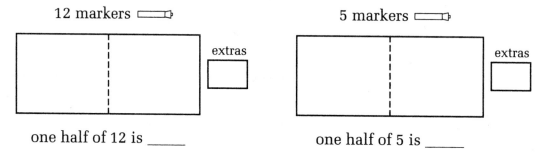

   one half of 12 is _____   one half of 5 is _____

3. Two fact family number sentences are 8 + 9 = 17 and 17 − 9 = 8. Write the other two fact family number sentences.

   _____   _____

4. How much money is this? _____

5. Find the answers.

   $$\begin{array}{r} 2\,3\,¢ \\ 4\,8\,¢ \\ +\,1\,7\,¢ \\ \hline \end{array}$$
   $$\begin{array}{r} 6\,5 \\ +\,7\,3 \\ \hline \end{array}$$

   9 × 10 = _____   10 − 6 = _____

   13 − 6 = _____   17 − 8 = _____

$$\begin{array}{r} 8 \\ \times\ 10 \\ \hline \end{array} \qquad \begin{array}{r} 10 \\ \times\ 4 \\ \hline \end{array} \qquad \begin{array}{r} 7 \\ \times\ 10 \\ \hline \end{array} \qquad \begin{array}{r} 5 \\ \times\ 10 \\ \hline \end{array} \qquad \begin{array}{r} 10 \\ \times\ 2 \\ \hline \end{array}$$

$$\begin{array}{r} 6 \\ \times\ 10 \\ \hline \end{array} \qquad \begin{array}{r} 10 \\ \times\ 1 \\ \hline \end{array} \qquad \begin{array}{r} 10 \\ \times\ 3 \\ \hline \end{array} \qquad \begin{array}{r} 9 \\ \times\ 10 \\ \hline \end{array} \qquad \begin{array}{r} 10 \\ \times\ 6 \\ \hline \end{array}$$

$$\begin{array}{r} 10 \\ \times\ 10 \\ \hline \end{array} \qquad \begin{array}{r} 10 \\ \times\ 5 \\ \hline \end{array} \qquad \begin{array}{r} 2 \\ \times\ 10 \\ \hline \end{array} \qquad \begin{array}{r} 10 \\ \times\ 8 \\ \hline \end{array} \qquad \begin{array}{r} 6 \\ \times\ 10 \\ \hline \end{array}$$

$$\begin{array}{r} 3 \\ \times\ 10 \\ \hline \end{array} \qquad \begin{array}{r} 10 \\ \times\ 7 \\ \hline \end{array} \qquad \begin{array}{r} 0 \\ \times\ 10 \\ \hline \end{array} \qquad \begin{array}{r} 6 \\ \times\ 10 \\ \hline \end{array} \qquad \begin{array}{r} 10 \\ \times\ 9 \\ \hline \end{array}$$

$$\begin{array}{r} 8 \\ \times\ 10 \\ \hline \end{array} \qquad \begin{array}{r} 10 \\ \times\ 2 \\ \hline \end{array} \qquad \begin{array}{r} 4 \\ \times\ 10 \\ \hline \end{array} \qquad \begin{array}{r} 10 \\ \times\ 0 \\ \hline \end{array} \qquad \begin{array}{r} 7 \\ \times\ 10 \\ \hline \end{array}$$

Score: _____

2-99Fa

Name •
(Draw a 4" line segment.)

Date •
(Draw a line segment 2" shorter than the line segment for your name.)

1. Fourteen children were in the gym. Twenty-five children from Room 12 joined them. Ten minutes later fifteen children from Room 6 arrived. How many children are in the gym now?

Number sentence _____ Answer _____

2. Show how the children will share the markers equally.

9 markers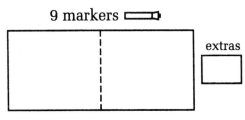

extras

14 markers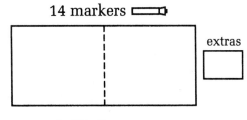

extras

one half of 9 is _____   one half of 14 is _____

3. What would be a good estimate of the height of a desk in your classroom?

5 feet 1 inch   1 foot 2 inches   2 feet 1 inch   12 feet 2 inches

4. What fractional part of each shape is shaded?

 _____   _____

5. How much money is this? Write the amount two ways. _____ _____

6. Find the products.

$9 \times 1 =$ _____ $7 \times 10 =$ _____ $5 \times 100 =$ _____ $14 \times 1 =$ _____

7. Find the answers.

$$\begin{array}{r} 8\,8 \\ +\ 3\,4 \\ \hline \end{array}$$

$$\begin{array}{r} 3\,7 \\ +\ 9\,2 \\ \hline \end{array}$$

$$\begin{array}{r} 1\,5 \\ 2\,3 \\ +\ 4\,7 \\ \hline \end{array}$$

Name _____   **LESSON 99B**

Date _____   **Math 2**

1. Eighteen children were in the lunch room. Twenty-two children from Room 7 arrived. Five minutes later, thirteen children from Room 21 joined them. How many children are in the lunch room now?

   Number sentence _____ Answer _____

2. Show how 2 children will share the markers equally.

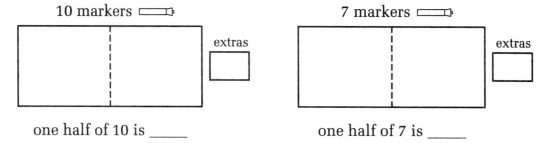

   one half of 10 is _____   one half of 7 is _____

3. What would be a good estimate of the height of a car?

   5 feet 1 inch   1 foot 2 inches   2 feet 1 inch   12 feet 2 inches

4. What fractional part of each shape is shaded?

 _____   _____

5. How much money is this? Write the amount two ways. _____ _____

6. Find the products.

   2 × 1 = _____   4 × 10 = _____   3 × 100 = _____   18 × 1 = _____

7. Find the answers.

```
                                                    2 5
     5 6                  2 9                        3 2
   + 6 3                + 3 8                      +   8
   ─────                ─────                      ─────
```

1. Sam has 18 stickers, Cedric has 27 stickers, and Tony has 32 stickers. How many stickers do the three boys have altogether?

   Number sentence _____ Answer _____

2. Write these numbers in expanded form.

   421 = _____   307 = _____

3. Find the answers.

   $3 \times 10 =$ _____ $8 \times 10 =$ _____ $10 - 7 =$ _____ $34 - 10 =$ _____

   $7 \times 10 =$ _____ $5 \times 10 =$ _____ $10 - 4 =$ _____ $49 + 10 =$ _____

4. Shade the graph to show that there are 20 children in Room 10.

   How many children are in Room 9? _____

   How many children are in Room 8? _____

   NUMBER OF CHILDREN IN EACH CLASSROOM

   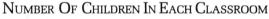

   Room 8

   Room 9

   Room 10

   0 2 4 6 8 10 12 14 16 18 20 22

   How many more children are in Room 10 than in Room 9? _____

5. It's afternoon. What time is it? _____

6. Find the answers.

   $$\begin{array}{r} 7\,4\,¢ \\ +\ 1\,7\,¢ \\ \hline \end{array}$$
   $$\begin{array}{r} 2\,3\,¢ \\ 4\,2\,¢ \\ +\ 1\,5\,¢ \\ \hline \end{array}$$
   $$\begin{array}{r} 3\,9\,¢ \\ 1\,9\,¢ \\ +\ 3\,4\,¢ \\ \hline \end{array}$$

Use 1" color tiles to cover each shape.

A

B

C

D

Area of each shape

A. _____ 1" color tiles

B. _____ 1" color tiles

C. _____ 1" color tiles

D. _____ 1" color tiles

$$
\begin{array}{r} 5 \\ -\ 1 \\ \hline \end{array}
\qquad
\begin{array}{r} 10 \\ -\ 6 \\ \hline \end{array}
\qquad
\begin{array}{r} 14 \\ -\ 9 \\ \hline \end{array}
\qquad
\begin{array}{r} 7 \\ -\ 6 \\ \hline \end{array}
\qquad
\begin{array}{r} 5 \\ -\ 3 \\ \hline \end{array}
$$

$$
\begin{array}{r} 13 \\ -\ 4 \\ \hline \end{array}
\qquad
\begin{array}{r} 9 \\ -\ 2 \\ \hline \end{array}
\qquad
\begin{array}{r} 8 \\ -\ 6 \\ \hline \end{array}
\qquad
\begin{array}{r} 10 \\ -\ 3 \\ \hline \end{array}
\qquad
\begin{array}{r} 16 \\ -\ 7 \\ \hline \end{array}
$$

$$
\begin{array}{r} 6 \\ -\ 3 \\ \hline \end{array}
\qquad
\begin{array}{r} 10 \\ -\ 2 \\ \hline \end{array}
\qquad
\begin{array}{r} 15 \\ -\ 9 \\ \hline \end{array}
\qquad
\begin{array}{r} 8 \\ -\ 7 \\ \hline \end{array}
\qquad
\begin{array}{r} 10 \\ -\ 7 \\ \hline \end{array}
$$

$$
\begin{array}{r} 4 \\ -\ 3 \\ \hline \end{array}
\qquad
\begin{array}{r} 17 \\ -\ 8 \\ \hline \end{array}
\qquad
\begin{array}{r} 10 \\ -\ 4 \\ \hline \end{array}
\qquad
\begin{array}{r} 7 \\ -\ 0 \\ \hline \end{array}
\qquad
\begin{array}{r} 9 \\ -\ 7 \\ \hline \end{array}
$$

$$
\begin{array}{r} 18 \\ -\ 9 \\ \hline \end{array}
\qquad
\begin{array}{r} 6 \\ -\ 5 \\ \hline \end{array}
\qquad
\begin{array}{r} 8 \\ -\ 2 \\ \hline \end{array}
\qquad
\begin{array}{r} 10 \\ -\ 8 \\ \hline \end{array}
\qquad
\begin{array}{r} 12 \\ -\ 3 \\ \hline \end{array}
$$

Score: _____

8 − 5	9 − 3	14 − 6	8 − 3	14 − 8
9 − 6	11 − 3	8 − 5	9 − 3	11 − 8
8 − 3	9 − 6	14 − 6	9 − 3	14 − 8
11 − 8	8 − 5	9 − 6	11 − 3	8 − 3
11 − 3	14 − 8	8 − 3	11 − 8	14 − 6

Score: _____

Name •
(Draw a $3\frac{1}{2}$" line segment.)

Date •
(Draw a $2\frac{1}{2}$" line segment.)

1. Catherine has 164 baseball cards, Steve has 247 baseball cards, Susan has 187 baseball cards, and Carl has 128 baseball cards.

   Who has the most cards? _____ Who has the fewest cards? _____

   Write the names of the children in order from the one who has the most cards to the one who has the fewest cards.

   _____   _____   _____   _____

2. Draw a picture to show three hundred twenty-one. (Use ☐ for 100, ☐ for 10, and ☐ for 1.)

   ┌───┐
   │   │
   │   │
   │   │
   └───┘

   Write this number in expanded form. _____
   Circle the number that shows three hundred twenty-one.

   3002001   321   30021   3021

3. I have 9 quarters. Draw the quarters.

   ┌───┐
   │   │
   │   │
   │   │
   └───┘

   How much money do I have? _____

4. Shade the thermometer to show 24°F.

5. It's morning. What time is it? _____

6. Find the products.

   $6 \times 10 =$ _____ $8 \times 1 =$ _____ $7 \times 100 =$ _____

Name _____

Date _____

1. Michael has 259 stamps in his stamp collection, Vera has 145 stamps, Crystal has 232 stamps, and Selby has 95 stamps.

   Who has the most stamps? _____ Who has the fewest stamps? _____

   Write the names of the children in order from the one who has the most stamps to the one who has the fewest stamps.

   _____   _____   _____   _____

2. Draw a picture to show two hundred fifty-three. (Use ☐ for 100, ☐ for 10, and ☐ for 1.)

   ┌───┐
   │   │
   │   │
   │   │
   └───┘

   Write this number in expanded form. _____
   Circle the number that shows two hundred fifty-three.

   20053   2053   200503   253

3. I have 7 quarters. Draw the quarters.

   ┌───┐
   │   │
   │   │
   │   │
   └───┘

   How much money do I have? _____

4. Shade the thermometer to show 86°F.

5. It's afternoon. What time is it? _____

6. Find the products.

   $9 \times 10 =$ _____ $3 \times 1 =$ _____ $6 \times 100 =$ _____

8 − 5	9 − 3	14 − 6	8 − 3	14 − 8
9 − 6	11 − 3	8 − 5	9 − 3	11 − 8
8 − 3	9 − 6	14 − 6	9 − 3	14 − 8
11 − 8	8 − 5	9 − 6	11 − 3	8 − 3
11 − 3	14 − 8	8 − 3	11 − 8	14 − 6

Score: _____

2-102Fa

Name •
(Draw a $2\frac{1}{2}$" line segment.)

Date •
(Draw a line segment 1" longer than the line segment for your name.)

1. The cost of a small notebook is 67¢. The cost of a pencil is 23¢. How much money does Stephen need to buy a small notebook and a pencil?

Number sentence _____ Answer _____

Draw the coins he could use to buy the notebook and pencil.

2. Show how to divide the pennies in half.

18 pennies (P)

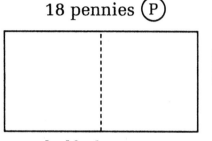

Extras

one half of 18 is _____

17 pennies (P)

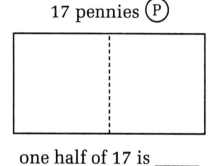

Extras

one half of 17 is _____

3. Fill in the correct comparison symbol (>, <, or =).

7 ☐ 9   17 ☐ 6   100 ☐ 200

4. Find the answers.

```
  8 4          2 5                              5 1            3
+ 3 4        + 1 7         8 × 100 = _____      1 9            7
-----        -----                            + 2 3           2
                           2 × 10 = _____      -----          4
                                                              8
                                                            + 5
                                                            -----
```

5. Fill in the missing numbers in the number patterns.

296, 297, 298, _____ , _____ , _____ , _____ , _____ , _____

_____ , _____ , _____ , 160, 170, 180, _____ , _____ , _____

Name _____

Date _____

1. The cost of a marker is 74¢. The cost of a small eraser is 19¢. How much money does DeAnna need to buy a marker and a small eraser?

    Number sentence _____ Answer _____

    Draw the coins she could use to buy the marker and eraser.

    ┌───┐
    │   │
    │   │
    │   │
    │   │
    └───┘

2. Show how to divide the pennies in half.

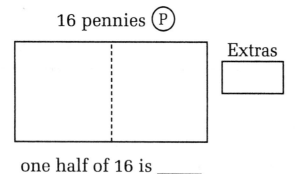

    16 pennies (P)

    Extras

    one half of 16 is _____

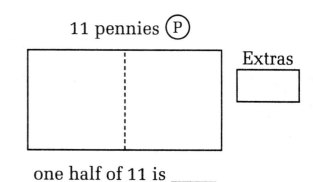

    11 pennies (P)

    Extras

    one half of 11 is _____

3. Fill in the correct comparison symbol (>, <, or =).

    12 ☐ 7   15 ☐ 18   230 ☐ 179

4. Find the answers.

    $$\begin{array}{r} 7\,4 \\ +\ 8\,5 \\ \hline \end{array} \qquad \begin{array}{r} 3\,6 \\ +\ 3\,9 \\ \hline \end{array}$$

    7 × 100 = _____

    3 × 10 = _____

    $$\begin{array}{r} 4\,6 \\ 2\,3 \\ +\ 1\,6 \\ \hline \end{array}$$

    $$\begin{array}{r} 3 \\ 1 \\ 7 \\ 8 \\ 6 \\ +\ 2 \\ \hline \end{array}$$

5. Fill in the missing numbers in the number patterns.

    305, 304, 303, _____ , _____ , _____ , _____ , _____ , _____

    _____ , _____ , _____ , _____ , _____ , _____ , 130, 140, 150

Cone	Cube	Sphere
Cylinder	Rectangular Solid	Pyramid

11	10	6	9	12
− 9	− 4	− 2	− 5	− 3

16	7	14	12	11
− 9	− 3	− 5	− 6	− 6

10	15	5	13	8
− 7	− 8	− 2	− 7	− 6

12	5	11	9	16
− 3	− 0	− 5	− 2	− 7

15	8	15	9	7
− 9	− 1	− 7	− 9	− 4

Score: _____

Name _____

Add it Up

Round 1	Round 2	Round 3

Dollars	Dimes	Pennies		Dollars	Dimes	Pennies		Dollars	Dimes	Pennies

Amount Won

Dollars	Dimes	Pennies	
			Round 1
			Round 2
			Round 3
			Grand Total

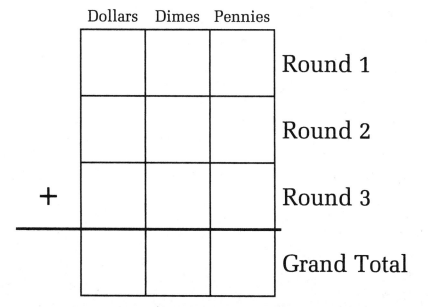

5 + 4	4 + 6	2 + 3	6 + 8	5 + 0	0 + 9	4 + 8	5 + 6	1 + 3	6 + 1
2 + 5	0 + 8	6 + 7	0 + 3	2 + 9	8 + 8	6 + 0	1 + 9	6 + 9	8 + 4
1 + 6	9 + 8	1 + 5	4 + 9	8 + 6	2 + 4	7 + 9	8 + 3	4 + 3	0 + 4
7 + 3	3 + 2	7 + 0	7 + 2	1 + 4	6 + 5	3 + 6	3 + 0	8 + 0	9 + 7
9 + 9	7 + 8	7 + 4	9 + 5	5 + 7	1 + 8	0 + 1	8 + 9	2 + 7	7 + 5
0 + 7	6 + 6	3 + 3	2 + 6	6 + 2	9 + 2	5 + 8	4 + 5	9 + 3	3 + 1
5 + 1	4 + 1	8 + 1	3 + 4	0 + 0	4 + 4	9 + 6	1 + 2	5 + 9	2 + 8
6 + 4	8 + 7	0 + 6	7 + 6	1 + 7	3 + 7	9 + 0	4 + 7	0 + 2	5 + 3
2 + 2	2 + 0	3 + 9	5 + 5	3 + 5	0 + 5	7 + 7	2 + 6	3 + 8	4 + 0
9 + 1	9 + 4	5 + 2	1 + 0	8 + 2	6 + 3	4 + 2	7 + 1	1 + 1	8 + 5

Name •————————————•

(Measure this line segment using inches. _____")

Date •————————————•

(Measure this line segment using inches. _____")

1. There are 25 children in Room 12. Eighteen of those children chose math as their favorite subject. There are 24 children in Room 14. Nineteen of those children chose math as their favorite subject. Altogether, how many children chose math as their favorite subject?

   Number sentence _____ Answer _____

2. Fill in the correct comparison symbol (>, <, or =).

   4 + 2 ☐ 7 − 1   4 + 4 ☐ 4 + 5   7 − 2 ☐ 4

3. Write a mixed number to show how many squares are shaded.

       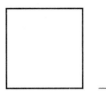 _____

4. Write these numbers in order from least to greatest.

   | 265   391   319   256 | ____ ____ ____ ____

                                   least   greatest

5. How much money is this?

   Write the amount two ways. _____ _____

6. Find the answers.

   ```
            4 2              3 5
     5 9    8 7              5 4
   + 7 3  + 2 1            + 6 9
   -----  -----            -----
   ```

1. There are 28 children in Room 17. Twenty-one of those children chose summer as their favorite season. There are 26 children in Room 18. Nineteen of those children chose summer as their favorite season. Altogether, how many children chose summer as their favorite season?

   Number sentence _____ Answer _____

2. Fill in the correct comparison symbol (>, <, or =).

   $4 - 3$ ☐ $7 - 5$ $6 + 6$ ☐ $9 + 3$ $8 + 3$ ☐ $4 + 6$

3. Write a mixed number to show how many circles are shaded.

         _____

4. Write these numbers in order from least to greatest.

   | 452   573   425   537 |

   _____ _____ _____ _____
   least   greatest

5. How much money is this?

   Write the amount two ways. _____ _____

6. Find the answers.

```
                53              79
   4 6          2 0             2 7
 + 9 2        + 3 8           + 5 3
 _____        _____           _____
```

Name •
(Draw a 4-inch line segment.)

Date •
(Draw a $1\frac{1}{2}$" line segment.)

1. Fred has 14 baseball cards. Show how he will share them equally with his brother.

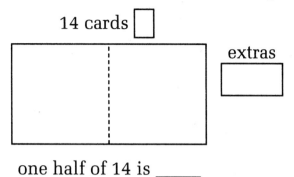

14 cards ☐

extras

one half of 14 is _____

How many baseball cards will each boy have? _____

2. About how tall are you? _____

3. Measure these line segments using inches.

•————————• _____"

•————————————————————————• _____"

4. I have 2 dimes, 3 nickels, and 7 pennies. Draw the coins. How much money is this?

Write the amount two ways. _____ _____

5. Color $2\frac{1}{4}$ circles.

◯ ◯ ◯ ◯

6. Find the answers.

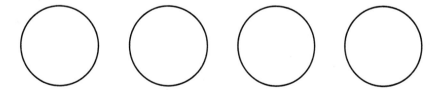

$$\begin{array}{r} 6\,5 \\ +\ 4\,8 \\ \hline \end{array}$$

$$\begin{array}{r} 5\,7 \\ +\ 9\,2 \\ \hline \end{array}$$

$$\begin{array}{r} 1\,4\,¢ \\ 2\,3\,¢ \\ +\ 3\,6\,¢ \\ \hline \end{array}$$

$62¢ + 18¢$

8 − 5	9 − 3	14 − 6	8 − 3	14 − 8
9 − 6	11 − 3	8 − 5	9 − 3	11 − 8
8 − 3	9 − 6	14 − 6	9 − 3	14 − 8
11 − 8	8 − 5	9 − 6	11 − 3	8 − 3
11 − 3	14 − 8	8 − 3	11 − 8	14 − 6

Score: _____

Name ●
(Draw a 9 cm line segment.)

Date ●————————————————————————————●

(Measure this line segment to the nearest centimeter. _____ cm)

1. Erica went to a party at 11:00 a.m. She left when the party was over at 2:00 p.m.

   How long was she at the party? _____

2. Draw a picture to show one hundred thirteen. (Use for 100, for 10, and for 1.)

   ┌───┐
   │   │
   │   │
   │   │
   │   │
   └───┘

   Write the number in expanded form. _____
   Circle the number that shows one hundred thirteen.

       10013   113   1013   100103

3. Color the cone yellow.

   Color the pyramid blue.

   Color the rectangular solid red.

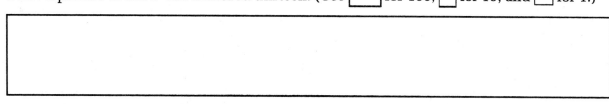

4. I have 10 quarters. Draw the coins. How much money do I have? _____

   ┌───┐
   │   │
   │   │
   │   │
   │   │
   └───┘

5. Fill in the missing numbers.

   $1 \times \boxed{} = 9$ $\boxed{} \times 10 = 20$ $3 \times \boxed{} = 300$

6. Find the answers.

       $64 + 73$ $68 + 7 + 13$ $29 + 73 + 21$

Name _____

Date _____

1. Luis went to visit his grandfather at 4:00 p.m. He left for home at 8:00 p.m.

   How long was he at his grandfather's? _____

2. Draw a picture to show three hundred twenty-four. (Use 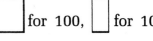 for 100, for 10, and for 1.)

   ┌───┐
   │   │
   │   │
   │   │
   │   │
   └───┘

   Write the number in expanded form. _____
   Circle the number that shows three hundred twenty-four.

       3204   324   30024   300204

3. Color the sphere orange.

   Color the cylinder green.

   Color the cube purple.

4. I have 8 quarters. Draw the coins. How much money do I have? _____

   ┌───┐
   │   │
   │   │
   │   │
   └───┘

5. Fill in the missing numbers.

   $4 \times \boxed{} = 40$ $\boxed{} \times 100 = 900$ $1 \times \boxed{} = 8$

6. Find the answers.
       84 + 65   24 + 8 + 56   73 + 46 + 31

3 × 5	5 × 5	1 × 5	7 × 5	5 × 4
5 × 6	0 × 5	9 × 5	5 × 2	5 × 8
0 × 5	5 × 9	4 × 5	5 × 2	7 × 5
5 × 6	5 × 1	5 × 5	8 × 5	3 × 5
2 × 5	5 × 7	5 × 3	5 × 8	6 × 5

Score: _____

2-106Fa

Name •
    (Draw a 7 cm line segment.)

Date •————————————————•

    (Measure this line segment using centimeters. _____ cm)

1. Leah said that whenever she adds two odd numbers the answer is always an even number. Add 3 pairs of odd numbers to see if she is right.

  ☐ + ☐ = ☐   ☐ + ☐ = ☐   ☐ + ☐ = ☐
  odd   odd ___   odd   odd ___   odd   odd ___

2. Show how to share the markers equally.

    13 markers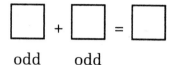

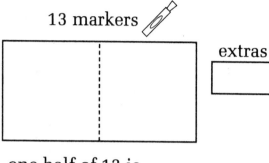   extras ☐

    8 markers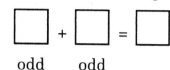

extras ☐

  one half of 13 is _____   one half of 8 is _____

3. Use the clues to write the children's names on the Venn diagram.
Sue has only a dog.
Mary has a cat and a dog.
Peter has only a cat.
Mark has both pets.
Sam has only a cat.

  How many children have a cat? _____

  How many children have only a dog? _____

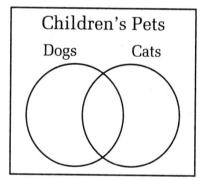

Children's Pets

Dogs   Cats

4. Find the products.

5	5	5	5	5	5	5	5	5	5	5
× 2	× 7	× 5	× 1	× 8	× 10	× 3	× 0	× 4	× 9	× 6

5. Find the answers.

    2 5 ¢   9 5   63 + 97   16 + 86
    3 7 ¢   9 2
  + 1 8 ¢   + 2 1

2-106Wa

1. Martell said that whenever he adds two even numbers the answer is always an even number. Add 3 pairs of even numbers to see if he is right.

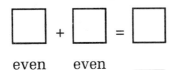 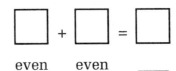 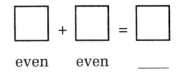

  even   even ____   even   even ____   even   even ____

2. Show how to share the pencils equally.

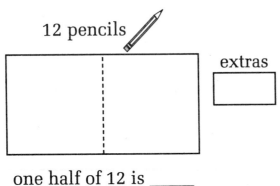 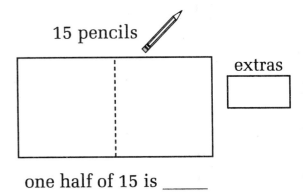

one half of 12 is _____   one half of 15 is _____

3. Use the clues to write the children's names on the Venn diagram.
Bob has fish and birds.
Tom has only a bird.
Carol has both pets.
Tim has only a bird.
Frank has only fish for pets.
Karen has only a bird.

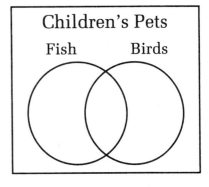

How many children have birds? _____

How many children have only fish? _____

4. Fill in the missing numbers.

5	5	5	5	5	5	5	5
× ☐	× ☐	× ☐	× ☐	× ☐	× ☐	× ☐	× ☐
15	20	40	0	25	50	5	45

5. Find the answers.

$$\begin{array}{r} 4\,6\,¢ \\ 1\,9\,¢ \\ +\,2\,5\,¢ \\ \hline \end{array} \qquad \begin{array}{r} 8\,4 \\ 7\,3 \\ +\,6\,1 \\ \hline \end{array} \qquad 86 + 34 \qquad 17 + 97$$

Name _____

3 × 5	5 × 5	1 × 5	7 × 5	5 × 4
5 × 6	0 × 5	9 × 5	5 × 2	5 × 8
0 × 5	5 × 9	4 × 5	5 × 2	7 × 5
5 × 6	5 × 1	5 × 5	8 × 5	3 × 5
2 × 5	5 × 7	5 × 3	5 × 8	6 × 5

Score: _____

Name ●

(Draw an 11 cm line segment.)

Date ●————————————————————●

(Measure this line segment using centimeters. _____ cm)

1. Ahmad put the peanuts in groups of 10. When he finished, he counted four groups of peanuts. Draw a picture and write a number sentence to show how many peanuts he has.

    ┌───┐
    │   │
    │   │
    │   │
    │   │
    └───┘

    _____ groups of _____ peanuts.   Number sentence _____

    How many peanuts does he have? _____

2. It's morning.
    What time is it? _____

3. Color the cubes red.
    Color the cylinders yellow.
    Color the pyramids blue.
    Shade the graph to show the number of cylinders, cubes, and pyramids.

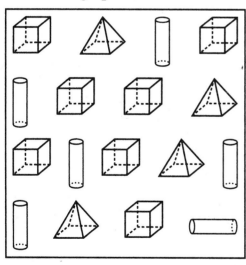

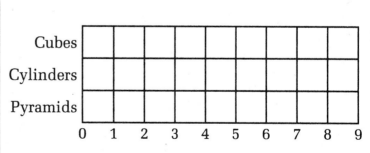

4. Find the answers.

    $7 \times 5 =$ _____ $3 \times 10 =$ _____ $24 + 97 =$ _____   7 8
                                                                                           2 4
    $4 \times 5 =$ _____ $52 - 10 =$ _____ $6 \times 100 =$ _____ $\underline{+\ 3\ 2}$

    $2 + 6 + 3 + 7 + 4 =$ _____

Name _____

Date _____

1. Justin put the paper clips in groups of 10. When he finished, he counted six groups of paper clips. Draw a picture and write a number sentence to show how many paper clips he has.

```
+-------------------------------------------------+
|                                                 |
|                                                 |
|                                                 |
|                                                 |
|                                                 |
+-------------------------------------------------+
```

_____ groups of _____ paper clips.   Number sentence _____

How many paper clips does he have? _____

2. It's afternoon.
   What time is it? _____

3. Color the spheres yellow.
   Color the rectangular solids blue.
   Color the cones red.
   Shade the graph to show the number of spheres, rectangular solids, and cones.

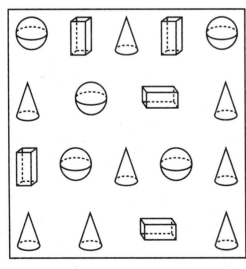

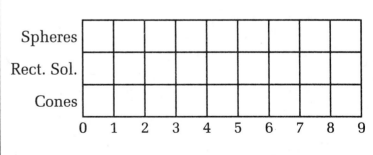

Spheres
Rect. Sol.
Cones

0 1 2 3 4 5 6 7 8 9

4. Find the answers.

$9 \times 5 =$ _____ $7 \times 10 =$ _____ $75 + 47 =$ _____

$6 \times 5 =$ _____ $63 - 10 =$ _____ $8 \times 100 =$ _____

$4 + 2 + 9 + 3 + 1 + 6 =$ _____

```
   8 4
   9 3
+  1 6
------
```

11 − 4	12 − 5	12 − 8	13 − 5	11 − 7
13 − 8	12 − 4	12 − 7	11 − 4	12 − 8
11 − 7	12 − 5	12 − 4	11 − 7	13 − 8
11 − 4	12 − 8	13 − 5	11 − 7	12 − 4
13 − 8	12 − 7	12 − 8	13 − 5	11 − 7

Score: _____

Name •
(Draw an 11 cm line segment.)

Date •————————————————————————•

(Measure this line segment using centimeters. _____ cm)

1. The grade 2 children at Emerson School collected cans for recycling. During the first week they collected 37 cans, during the second week they collected 88 cans, and during the third week they collected 96 cans. How many cans did they collect during the first two weeks?

   Number sentence _____ Answer _____

   During which week were the most cans collected? _____

2. Draw a picture to show three hundred fifteen. (Use 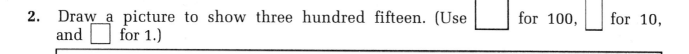 for 100, ☐ for 10, and ☐ for 1.)

   [blank box]

   Write this number in expanded form. _____

   Write three hundred fifteen using digits. _____

3. Show how to share the pattern blocks equally.

   13 green pattern blocks △

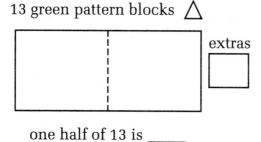

   one half of 13 is _____

   16 orange pattern blocks ☐

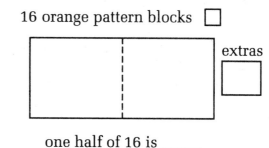

   one half of 16 is _____

4. Circle the ones that are the same as 56¢.

   6 dimes 5 pennies   56 pennies

   4 dimes 16 pennies   6 pennies 5 dimes

5. Find the answers.

   4 × 5 = _____   6 × 100 = _____   5 9
                                               + 4 1
                                               ———

                                                3 8
   9 × 5 = _____   0 × 5 = _____   + 9 1
                                               ———

1. The grade 2 children in Mrs. Haller's class and Mrs. Carrell's class collected bottles for recycling. During the first week they collected 63 bottles, during the second week they collected 49 bottles, and during the third week they collected 32 bottles. How many bottles did they collect during the first two weeks?

   Number sentence _____ Answer _____

   During which week were the most bottles collected? _____

2. Draw a picture to show two hundred sixteen. (Use ☐ for 100, ☐ for 10, and ☐ for 1.)

   Write this number in expanded form. _____

   Write two hundred sixteen using digits. _____

3. Show how to share the pattern blocks equally.

   17 green pattern blocks △

   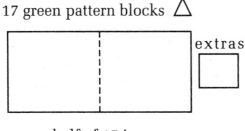

   one half of 17 is _____

   14 orange pattern blocks ☐

   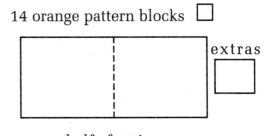

   one half of 14 is _____

4. Circle the ones that are the same as 42¢.

   3 dimes 12 pennies   2 pennies 4 dimes

   2 dimes 4 pennies   42 dimes

5. Find the answers.

   6 × 5 = _____   9 × 100 = _____   3 7
                                                   + 6 3
                                                   _____

   8 × 5 = _____   0 × 10 = _____   7 2
                                                   + 8 3
                                                   _____

11	12	12	13	11
− 4	− 5	− 8	− 5	− 7

13	12	12	11	12
− 8	− 4	− 7	− 4	− 8

11	12	12	11	13
− 7	− 5	− 4	− 7	− 8

11	12	13	11	12
− 4	− 8	− 5	− 7	− 4

13	12	12	13	11
− 8	− 7	− 8	− 5	− 7

Score: _____

Name ●

(Draw a 9 cm line segment.)

Date ●————————————————●

(Measure this line segment using centimeters. _____ cm)

1. The children in Room 6 collected 16 quarters. They spent 9 quarters for new markers for the classroom. Draw a picture and write a number sentence to show what happened.

Number sentence _____

How many quarters do they have left? _____ How much money is that? _____

2. Write the fact family number sentences for 4, 5, and 9.

_____   _____

_____   _____

3. Show 94°F on the thermometer.

4. Find each answer.

$$\begin{array}{r} 5\ 2¢ \\ -\ 2\ 4¢ \\ \hline \end{array}$$
$$\begin{array}{r} 3\ 6¢ \\ -\ 2\ 3¢ \\ \hline \end{array}$$
$$\begin{array}{r} 5\ 8¢ \\ +\ 3\ 6¢ \\ \hline \end{array}$$

5. Write four hundred twenty using digits. _____

Write this number in expanded form. _____

6. Draw a line of symmetry in each shape. Color one side.

 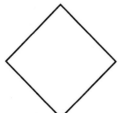 

What fractional part of each shape did you color? _____

Thermometer showing scale from −20°F to 100°F:
100°F
90°F
80°F
70°F
60°F
50°F
40°F
30°F
20°F
10°F
0°F
−10°F
−20°F

1. Sharon had 5 quarters. Her sister gave her nine more quarters. Draw a picture and write a number sentence to show what happened.

   Number sentence _____

   How many quarters does Sharon have now? _____

   How much money is that? _____

2. Write the fact family number sentences for 6, 7, and 13.

   _____   _____

   _____   _____

3. Show 26°F on the thermometer.

4. Find each answer.

   $$\begin{array}{r} 6\ 3¢ \\ -\ 4\ 7¢ \\ \hline \end{array}$$ $$\begin{array}{r} 7\ 5¢ \\ -\ 6\ 1¢ \\ \hline \end{array}$$ $$\begin{array}{r} 4\ 7¢ \\ +\ 1\ 6¢ \\ \hline \end{array}$$

5. Write five hundred seven using digits. _____

   Write this number in expanded form. _____

6. Draw a line of symmetry in each shape. Color one side.

    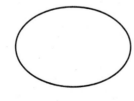 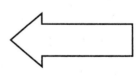

   What fractional part of each shape did you color? _____

100°F
90°F
80°F
70°F
60°F
50°F
40°F
30°F
20°F
10°F
0°F
–10°F
–20°F

1. There are 22 children in Room 7. Twelve of these children are wearing sneakers. There are 24 children in Room 8. Fifteen of these children are wearing sneakers. Altogether, how many children are wearing sneakers?

   Number sentence _____ Answer _____

2. Carla has 10 quarters. Draw the quarters.

   How much money is that? _____

3. Show how to share the balloons equally.

   One half of 12 is _____   One half of 9 is _____

4. Draw a picture to show four hundred fifty-two. (Use ☐ for 100, ☐ for 10, and ☐ for 1.)

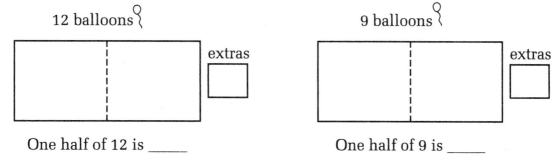

   Write this number in expanded form. _____

   Write four hundred fifty-two using digits. _____

5. Find the answers.

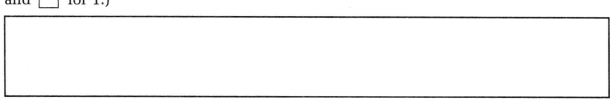

   $4 \times 10 =$ _____ $9 \times 100 =$ _____

   $7 \times 10 =$ _____ $10 - 6 =$ _____

$$\begin{array}{r} 7\,8 \\ +\ 3\,7 \\ \hline \end{array} \qquad \begin{array}{r} 9\,2 \\ +\ 4\,9 \\ \hline \end{array} \qquad \begin{array}{r} 3\,9 \\ 1\,6 \\ +\ 2\,3 \\ \hline \end{array}$$

Cover each shape using tangram pieces.

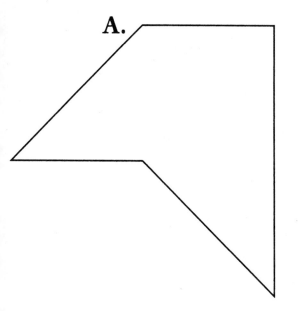

A.

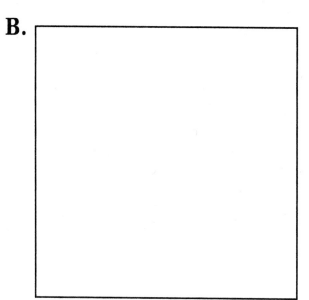

B.

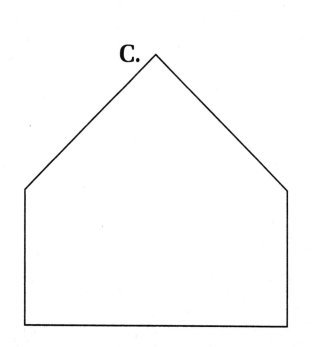

C.

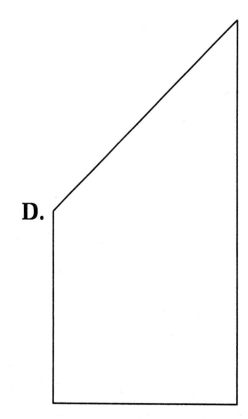

D.

$$\begin{array}{r} 11 \\ -\ 9 \\ \hline \end{array} \qquad \begin{array}{r} 10 \\ -\ 4 \\ \hline \end{array} \qquad \begin{array}{r} 6 \\ -\ 2 \\ \hline \end{array} \qquad \begin{array}{r} 9 \\ -\ 5 \\ \hline \end{array} \qquad \begin{array}{r} 12 \\ -\ 3 \\ \hline \end{array}$$

$$\begin{array}{r} 16 \\ -\ 9 \\ \hline \end{array} \qquad \begin{array}{r} 7 \\ -\ 3 \\ \hline \end{array} \qquad \begin{array}{r} 14 \\ -\ 5 \\ \hline \end{array} \qquad \begin{array}{r} 12 \\ -\ 6 \\ \hline \end{array} \qquad \begin{array}{r} 11 \\ -\ 6 \\ \hline \end{array}$$

$$\begin{array}{r} 10 \\ -\ 7 \\ \hline \end{array} \qquad \begin{array}{r} 15 \\ -\ 8 \\ \hline \end{array} \qquad \begin{array}{r} 5 \\ -\ 2 \\ \hline \end{array} \qquad \begin{array}{r} 13 \\ -\ 7 \\ \hline \end{array} \qquad \begin{array}{r} 8 \\ -\ 6 \\ \hline \end{array}$$

$$\begin{array}{r} 12 \\ -\ 3 \\ \hline \end{array} \qquad \begin{array}{r} 5 \\ -\ 0 \\ \hline \end{array} \qquad \begin{array}{r} 11 \\ -\ 5 \\ \hline \end{array} \qquad \begin{array}{r} 9 \\ -\ 2 \\ \hline \end{array} \qquad \begin{array}{r} 16 \\ -\ 7 \\ \hline \end{array}$$

$$\begin{array}{r} 15 \\ -\ 9 \\ \hline \end{array} \qquad \begin{array}{r} 8 \\ -\ 1 \\ \hline \end{array} \qquad \begin{array}{r} 15 \\ -\ 7 \\ \hline \end{array} \qquad \begin{array}{r} 9 \\ -\ 9 \\ \hline \end{array} \qquad \begin{array}{r} 7 \\ -\ 4 \\ \hline \end{array}$$

Score: _____

3 × 5	5 × 5	1 × 5	7 × 5	5 × 4
5 × 6	0 × 5	9 × 5	5 × 2	5 × 8
0 × 5	5 × 9	4 × 5	5 × 2	7 × 5
5 × 6	5 × 1	5 × 5	8 × 5	3 × 5
2 × 5	5 × 7	5 × 3	5 × 8	6 × 5

Score: _____

Name _____ •
(Draw a 10 cm line segment.)

Date •————————————•

(Measure this line segment using centimeters. _____ cm)

1. There are 16 markers in a package. Kristina will share them equally with her cousin Michael. Show how the children will share the markers.

    How many markers will each child have? _____

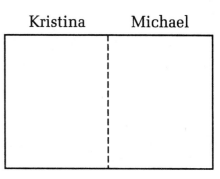

2. Color $3\frac{3}{4}$ squares.

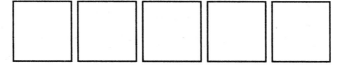

3. Write the fact family number sentences for 7, 16, and 9.

    _____   _____

    _____   _____

4. Find the answers.

    $$\begin{array}{r} 6\ 3\ ¢ \\ -\ 3\ 7\ ¢ \\ \hline \end{array}$$ $$\begin{array}{r} 4\ 8\ ¢ \\ -\ 1\ 6\ ¢ \\ \hline \end{array}$$ $$\begin{array}{r} 5\ 0\ ¢ \\ -\ 3\ 4\ ¢ \\ \hline \end{array}$$

5. This is the time I get up in the morning.

    What time is it? _____

6. Find the answers.

    $6 \times 5 =$ _____ $4 \times 10 =$ _____ $$\begin{array}{r} 2\ 4 \\ 3\ 6 \\ +\ 5\ 9 \\ \hline \end{array}$$ $$\begin{array}{r} 4\ 8 \\ 9\ 3 \\ +\ 1\ 6 \\ \hline \end{array}$$

    $7 \times 1 =$ _____ $9 \times 5 =$ _____

    $3 \times 100 =$ _____ $0 \times 1 =$ _____

1. There are 10 postcards in a package. Bruce will share them equally with his sister Sarah. Show how the children will share the postcards.

   How many postcards will each child have? _____

   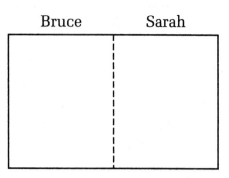

2. Color $4\frac{1}{4}$ squares.

3. Write the fact family number sentences for 12, 3, and 9.

   _____   _____

   _____   _____

4. Find the answers.

   $$\begin{array}{r} 5\,1\,¢ \\ -\ 1\,7\,¢ \\ \hline \end{array}$$ $$\begin{array}{r} 7\,0\,¢ \\ -\ 5\,2\,¢ \\ \hline \end{array}$$ $$\begin{array}{r} 6\,7\,¢ \\ -\ 4\,3\,¢ \\ \hline \end{array}$$

5. This is the time I eat lunch.

   What time is it? _____

6. Find the answers.

   $4 \times 5 =$ _____ $6 \times 10 =$ _____ $$\begin{array}{r} 1\,9 \\ 2\,3 \\ +\ 8\,2 \\ \hline \end{array}$$ $$\begin{array}{r} 2\,1 \\ 5\,3 \\ +\ 6\,4 \\ \hline \end{array}$$

   $0 \times 10 =$ _____ $7 \times 5 =$ _____

   $7 \times 100 =$ _____ $4 \times 1 =$ _____

11 − 4	12 − 5	12 − 8	13 − 5	11 − 7
13 − 8	12 − 4	12 − 7	11 − 4	12 − 8
11 − 7	12 − 5	12 − 4	11 − 7	13 − 8
11 − 4	12 − 8	13 − 5	11 − 7	12 − 4
13 − 8	12 − 7	12 − 8	13 − 5	11 − 7

Score: _____

(Draw a 12 cm line segment.)

(Measure this line segment using centimeters. _____ cm)

1. The children in Mrs. Conte's class planted 18 tomato plants and 16 pepper plants. The children in Mrs. Mancano's class planted 14 tomato plants and 15 squash plants. How many tomato plants did they plant altogether?

   Number sentence _____

   Answer _____

2. About how much might the lunch box of a child in your classroom weigh?

   200 pounds   2 pounds   40 pounds   20 pounds

3. Draw 8 squares. Color half of the squares red.

   How many squares did you color? _____

4. Find the answers.

$$\begin{array}{r} 7\ 9\ ¢ \\ -\ 3\ 4\ ¢ \\ \hline \end{array} \qquad \begin{array}{r} 5\ 6\ ¢ \\ -\ 1\ 8\ ¢ \\ \hline \end{array} \qquad \begin{array}{r} 8\ 0\ ¢ \\ -\ 2\ 7\ ¢ \\ \hline \end{array}$$

5. The children in Mrs. McCluckie's class counted eleven blue cars, eight red cars, and four grey cars in the parking lot.

   Shade the graph to show the colors of the cars.

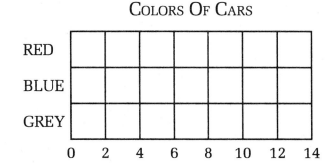

COLORS OF CARS

RED
BLUE
GREY

0   2   4   6   8   10   12   14

   How many more blue cars than grey cars did they count? _____

6. Find the answers.

$$\begin{array}{r} 3\ 5 \\ 4\ 3 \\ +\ 1\ 4 \\ \hline \end{array}$$

   $2 \times 10 =$ _____ $7 \times 5 =$ _____ $5 \times 1 =$ _____

   $8 \times 100 =$ _____ $3 + 9 + 2 + 7 + 8 + 1 + 2 =$ _____

1. The children in Mrs. Ley's class planted 24 geraniums and 36 marigold plants. The children in Mrs. Delmonte's class planted 38 geraniums and 20 marigold plants. How many geraniums did the children plant altogether?

    Number sentence _____

    Answer _____

2. About how much would a gallon of milk weigh?

    80 pounds   30 pounds   8 pounds   1 pound

3. Draw 10 triangles. Color half of the triangles.

    How many triangles did you color? _____

4. Find the answers.

$$84 ¢ - 57 ¢$$ $$56 ¢ - 32 ¢$$ $$60 ¢ - 13 ¢$$

5. The children in Mrs. Kasner's class counted seven blue cars, thirteen red cars, and eight grey cars in the parking lot.

    Shade the graph to show the colors of the cars.

    How many more red cars than grey cars did they count? _____

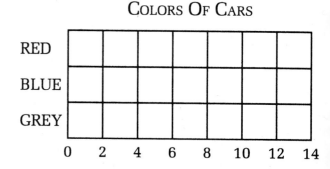

COLORS OF CARS

RED

BLUE

GREY

0   2   4   6   8   10   12   14

6. Find the answers.

    $6 \times 10 =$ _____ $8 \times 5 =$ _____ $3 \times 1 =$ _____

    $5 \times 100 =$ _____ $4 + 8 + 3 + 2 + 5 + 7 + 5 =$ _____

$$\begin{array}{r} 2\,9 \\ 3\,1 \\ +\,2\,8 \\ \hline \end{array}$$

Name _____

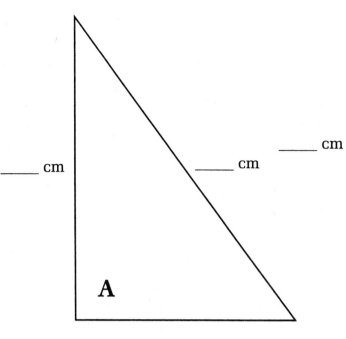

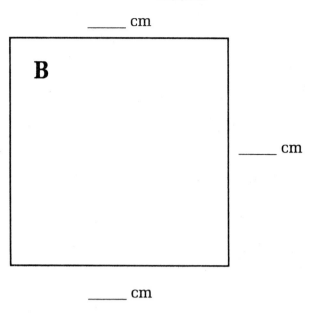

A

_____ cm

_____ cm

_____ cm

Perimeter = _____

B

_____ cm

_____ cm

_____ cm

_____ cm

Perimeter = _____

C

_____ cm

_____ cm

_____ cm

_____ cm

Perimeter = _____

D

_____ cm

_____ cm

_____ cm

_____ cm

Perimeter = _____

5 + 4	4 + 6	2 + 3	6 + 8	5 + 0	0 + 9	4 + 8	5 + 6	1 + 3	6 + 1
2 + 5	0 + 8	6 + 7	0 + 3	2 + 9	8 + 8	6 + 0	1 + 9	6 + 9	8 + 4
1 + 6	9 + 8	1 + 5	4 + 9	8 + 6	2 + 4	7 + 9	8 + 3	4 + 3	0 + 4
7 + 3	3 + 2	7 + 0	7 + 2	1 + 4	6 + 5	3 + 6	3 + 0	8 + 0	9 + 7
9 + 9	7 + 8	7 + 4	9 + 5	5 + 7	1 + 8	0 + 1	8 + 9	2 + 7	7 + 5
0 + 7	6 + 6	3 + 3	2 + 6	6 + 2	9 + 2	5 + 8	4 + 5	9 + 3	3 + 1
5 + 1	4 + 1	8 + 1	3 + 4	0 + 0	4 + 4	9 + 6	1 + 2	5 + 9	2 + 8
6 + 4	8 + 7	0 + 6	7 + 6	1 + 7	3 + 7	9 + 0	4 + 7	0 + 2	5 + 3
2 + 2	2 + 0	3 + 9	5 + 5	3 + 5	0 + 5	7 + 7	2 + 6	3 + 8	4 + 0
9 + 1	9 + 4	5 + 2	1 + 0	8 + 2	6 + 3	4 + 2	7 + 1	1 + 1	8 + 5

Name

(Draw an 8 cm line segment.)

Date

(Measure this line segment using centimeters. _____ cm)

1. Kyle tallied the number of children who said no. | ЈНТ ЈНТ ЈНТ |||

Sherry tallied the number of children who said yes. | ЈНТ ЈНТ ЈНТ ЈНТ ЈНТ ||

How many children said no? _____

How many children said yes? _____

How many children voted altogether? _____

2. Use the correct comparison symbol (>, <, or =).

14 ☐ 41   3 × 5 ☐ 5 + 5 + 5   28 + 30 ☐ 6 × 10

3. Measure each side of the triangle using centimeters.

What is the perimeter?

Number sentence _____

Perimeter _____

_____ cm

_____ cm   _____ cm

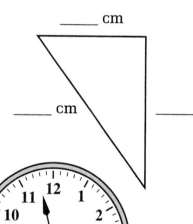

4. It's dark outside.

What time is it? _____

5. Write the answer for 20 + 7 + 300. _____

6. Find each answer.

```
   4 9          7 0          5 1          6 5
 - 2 6        - 2 3        - 3 8          2 9
 _____        _____        _____        + 5 1
                                        _____
```

Name _____

Date _____

1. Duane tallied the number of blue cars.

   Suzanne tallied the number of red cars.

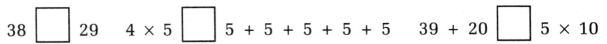

   How many blue cars did Duane count? _____

   How many red cars did Suzanne count? _____

   How many cars did the children count altogether? _____

2. Use the correct comparison symbol (>, <, or =).

   38 ⬜ 29   4 × 5 ⬜ 5 + 5 + 5 + 5 + 5   39 + 20 ⬜ 5 × 10

3. Chris measured the sides of a triangle and drew a small picture.

   What is the perimeter?

   Number sentence _____

   Perimeter _____

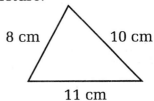

4. It's light outside.

   What time is it? _____

5. Write the answer for 6 + 200 + 80. _____

6. Find each answer.

   $$\begin{array}{r} 47 \\ -\ 19 \\ \hline \end{array} \qquad \begin{array}{r} 40 \\ -\ 28 \\ \hline \end{array} \qquad \begin{array}{r} 65 \\ -\ 43 \\ \hline \end{array} \qquad \begin{array}{r} 74 \\ 23 \\ +\ 34 \\ \hline \end{array}$$

12 − 4	8 − 3	9 − 6	11 − 8	12 − 5
14 − 6	11 − 4	13 − 5	12 − 8	9 − 3
11 − 7	13 − 8	12 − 7	8 − 5	14 − 8
11 − 3	9 − 6	12 − 4	13 − 5	11 − 8
14 − 6	8 − 3	11 − 4	12 − 8	12 − 5

Score: _____

Name •
(Draw a 10 cm line segment.)

Date •————————————————————————•

(Measure this line segment using centimeters. _____ cm)

1. There are 124 children in grade 1, 147 children in grade 2, and 119 children in grade 3.

   Which grade has the most children? _____

   Which grade has the fewest children? _____

   Write the names of the grades in order from the one that has the most children to the one that has the fewest children.

   _____   _____   _____

2. I have 4 dimes, 3 nickels, and 7 pennies. Draw the coins. How much money do I have? Write the amount two ways.

   _____   _____

3. Measure each side of the rectangle in Problem 2 using centimeters. Find the perimeter.

   Number sentence _____   What is the perimeter? _____

4. Fill in a number to make each number sentence true.

   ☐ < 6   13 < ☐   4 + 7 = 7 + ☐

5. The children in Miss Quinn's class made the following graph. Write something you know about the children.

   FAVORITE ICE CREAM FLAVORS

   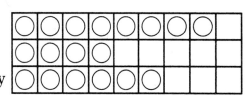

   _____

   _____

6. Find the answers.

   $$77 + 46 = \underline{\hphantom{000}} \qquad 9 + 88 = \underline{\hphantom{000}}$$

   $$\begin{array}{r} 8\,6 \\ -\,2\,7 \\ \hline \end{array} \qquad \begin{array}{r} 9\,8 \\ -\,3\,5 \\ \hline \end{array}$$

Name _____

Date _____

1. There are 195 children in grade 4, 215 children in grade 5, and 178 children in grade 6.

   Which grade has the most children? _____

   Which grade has the fewest children? _____

   Write the names of the grades in order from the one that has the most children to the one that has the fewest children.

   _____   _____   _____

2. I have 5 dimes, 3 nickels, and 8 pennies. Draw the coins. How much money do I have? Write the amount two ways.

   _____   _____

   7 cm

   3 cm

3. Someone measured each side of the rectangle in Problem 2 using centimeters. Find the perimeter.

   Number sentence _____   What is the perimeter? _____

4. Fill in a number to make each number sentence true.

   ☐ > 9   7 > ☐   8 + ☐ = 5 + 8

5. The children in Miss Padilla's class made the following graph. Write something you know about the children.

   _____

   _____

   FAVORITE ICE CREAM FLAVORS

   chocolate ◯◯◯◯

   vanilla   ◯◯◯◯◯

   strawberry ◯◯◯◯◯◯◯

6. Find the answers.

   86 + 35 = ____   7 + 94 = ____

   $\begin{array}{r} 9\ 1 \\ -\ 3\ 5 \\ \hline \end{array}$ $\begin{array}{r} 2\ 3 \\ -\ 1\ 1 \\ \hline \end{array}$

1. Barbara has 314 pennies, Celina has 276 pennies, Amber has 358 pennies, and Megan has 298 pennies.

   Who has the most pennies? _____   Who has the fewest pennies? _____

   Write the names of the children in order from the one who has the most pennies to the one who has the fewest pennies.

   _____ _____ _____ _____

2. Color the cone yellow.
   Color the sphere red.
   Color the cylinder blue.
   Color the cube green.

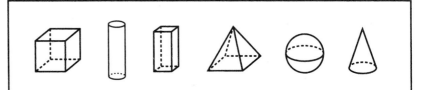

3. Use the correct comparison symbol (>, <, or =).

   16 ☐ 9   3 + 7 ☐ 10   8 + 1 ☐ 8 + 2

4. Five children have red lunch boxes.

   Twelve children have yellow lunch boxes.

   Eleven children have blue lunch boxes.

   Shade the graph to show the number of children with each color lunch box.

   LUNCH BOX COLORS

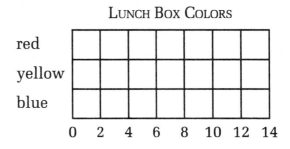

   red
   yellow
   blue

   0   2   4   6   8   10 12 14

5. Find the answers.

   6 × 100 = _____   7 × 5 = _____   6 7   7 3
                                                     4 3   9
   4 × 10 = _____   4 × 5 = _____   + 2 8   + 3 6
                                                    ———   ———
   7 × 100 = _____   8 × 1 = _____

12	8	9	11	12
− 4	− 3	− 6	− 8	− 5

14	11	13	12	9
− 6	− 4	− 5	− 8	− 3

11	13	12	8	14
− 7	− 8	− 7	− 5	− 8

11	9	12	13	11
− 3	− 6	− 4	− 5	− 8

14	8	11	12	12
− 6	− 3	− 4	− 8	− 5

Score: _____

Name •

(Draw a $3\frac{1}{2}$" line segment.)

Date •————————————•

(Measure this line segment using inches. _____ ")

1. There were a dozen children in the pool. How many children were in the pool? _____

    A half dozen of the children left the pool. How many children left the pool? _____

    Write a number sentence to show how many children are in the pool now.

    Number sentence _____ Answer _____

2. I have 9 quarters. Draw the coins. How much money do I have? _____

3. What is the perimeter of each shape?

    Shape A _____

    Shape B _____

    Shape A: 3", 4", 4", 6"

    Shape B: 5 cm, 7 cm, 10 cm, 3 cm

4. Use a crayon to trace the parallel line segments in each shape in Problem 3.

5. Color the pyramid red.
    Color the cylinder blue.
    Color the sphere yellow.

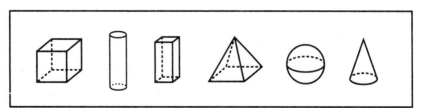

6. Find the answers.

    $4 \times 100 =$ _____ $2 \times 10 =$ _____

    $6 + 3 + 9 + 2 + 5 + 4 + 1 =$ _____

    $\begin{array}{r} 7\,4 \\ -\,4\,7 \\ \hline \end{array}$ $\begin{array}{r} 6\,3 \\ -\,4\,8 \\ \hline \end{array}$ $\begin{array}{r} 9\,6 \\ 2\,5 \\ +\,3\,2 \\ \hline \end{array}$

Name _____

Date _____

1. There were a half dozen children in the gym. How many children were in the gym? ____

   Another half dozen children joined them. How many children came into the gym? ____

   Write a number sentence to show how many children are in the gym now.

   Number sentence _____ Answer _____

2. I have 8 quarters. Draw the coins. How much money do I have? _____

3. What is the perimeter of each shape?

   Shape A _____

   Shape B _____

4. Use a crayon to trace the parallel line segments in each shape in Problem 3.

5. Color the cone green.
   Color the cube orange.
   Color the sphere purple.

   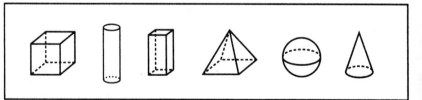

6. Find the answers.

   $6 \times 100 =$ _____ $5 \times 10 =$ _____

   $4 + 8 + 2 + 7 + 4 + 3 + 1 =$ _____

   $$\begin{array}{r} 5\ 1 \\ -\ 1\ 8 \\ \hline \end{array}$$

   $$\begin{array}{r} 7\ 3 \\ -\ 3\ 7 \\ \hline \end{array}$$

   $$\begin{array}{r} 7\ 2 \\ 2\ 4 \\ +\ 4\ 7 \\ \hline \end{array}$$

$$
\begin{array}{r} 6 \\ \times\ 2 \\ \hline \end{array}
\qquad
\begin{array}{r} 1 \\ \times\ 2 \\ \hline \end{array}
\qquad
\begin{array}{r} 9 \\ \times\ 2 \\ \hline \end{array}
\qquad
\begin{array}{r} 4 \\ \times\ 2 \\ \hline \end{array}
\qquad
\begin{array}{r} 7 \\ \times\ 2 \\ \hline \end{array}
$$

$$
\begin{array}{r} 3 \\ \times\ 2 \\ \hline \end{array}
\qquad
\begin{array}{r} 8 \\ \times\ 2 \\ \hline \end{array}
\qquad
\begin{array}{r} 2 \\ \times\ 2 \\ \hline \end{array}
\qquad
\begin{array}{r} 5 \\ \times\ 2 \\ \hline \end{array}
\qquad
\begin{array}{r} 0 \\ \times\ 2 \\ \hline \end{array}
$$

$$
\begin{array}{r} 2 \\ \times\ 2 \\ \hline \end{array}
\qquad
\begin{array}{r} 2 \\ \times\ 8 \\ \hline \end{array}
\qquad
\begin{array}{r} 2 \\ \times\ 1 \\ \hline \end{array}
\qquad
\begin{array}{r} 2 \\ \times\ 7 \\ \hline \end{array}
\qquad
\begin{array}{r} 2 \\ \times\ 5 \\ \hline \end{array}
$$

$$
\begin{array}{r} 2 \\ \times\ 0 \\ \hline \end{array}
\qquad
\begin{array}{r} 2 \\ \times\ 4 \\ \hline \end{array}
\qquad
\begin{array}{r} 2 \\ \times\ 6 \\ \hline \end{array}
\qquad
\begin{array}{r} 2 \\ \times\ 3 \\ \hline \end{array}
\qquad
\begin{array}{r} 2 \\ \times\ 9 \\ \hline \end{array}
$$

$$
\begin{array}{r} 5 \\ \times\ 2 \\ \hline \end{array}
\qquad
\begin{array}{r} 2 \\ \times\ 8 \\ \hline \end{array}
\qquad
\begin{array}{r} 6 \\ \times\ 2 \\ \hline \end{array}
\qquad
\begin{array}{r} 2 \\ \times\ 4 \\ \hline \end{array}
\qquad
\begin{array}{r} 1 \\ \times\ 2 \\ \hline \end{array}
$$

Score: _____

2-116Fa

Name **•**
(Draw a 12 cm line segment.)

Date **•————————————————————————•**
(Measure this line segment using centimeters. _____ cm)

1. Dolores has 3 dimes and 6 pennies. Francis has 7 pennies and 2 dimes.

    How much money does Dolores have? _____

    How much money does Francis have? _____

    How much money do they have altogether?

    Number sentence _____ Answer _____

2. Put these numbers in order from least to greatest.

    | 176 284 373 181 279 | ____ ____ ____ ____ ____

    least   greatest

3. Circle the letters that have parallel line segments.

    | A   E   L   M   V   Z |

4. Find the answers.

    $\begin{array}{cccccccccc} 2 & 2 & 2 & 2 & 2 & 2 & 2 & 2 & 2 & 2 & 2 \\ \times 4 & \times 8 & \times 3 & \times 7 & \times 5 & \times 9 & \times 1 & \times 6 & \times 2 & \times 0 & \times 10 \end{array}$

5. Calvin has four markers. Draw the markers. One marker is red. Color that marker.

    What fractional part of the markers is red? _____

6. Find the answers.

    $52 + 39 + 48$ $7 + 36$ $31 - 14$ $74 - 43$

1. Juan has 6 pennies and 4 dimes. Gary has 3 dimes and 9 pennies.

   How much money does Juan have? _____

   How much money does Gary have? _____

   How much money do they have altogether?

   Number sentence _____ Answer _____

2. Put these numbers in order from least to greatest.

   | 192 284 194 487 291 | ____   ____   ____   ____   ____

   least   greatest

3. Circle the letters that have parallel line segments.

   H Y I N T X

4. Fill in the missing numbers.

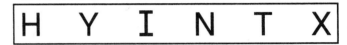

5. Steve has three markers. Draw the markers. One marker is green. Color that marker.

   What fractional part of the markers is green? _____

6. Find the answers.

   31 + 49 + 24   6 + 58   43 − 29   82 − 51

$$\begin{array}{r} 6 \\ \times\ 2 \\ \hline \end{array} \qquad \begin{array}{r} 1 \\ \times\ 2 \\ \hline \end{array} \qquad \begin{array}{r} 9 \\ \times\ 2 \\ \hline \end{array} \qquad \begin{array}{r} 4 \\ \times\ 2 \\ \hline \end{array} \qquad \begin{array}{r} 7 \\ \times\ 2 \\ \hline \end{array}$$

$$\begin{array}{r} 3 \\ \times\ 2 \\ \hline \end{array} \qquad \begin{array}{r} 8 \\ \times\ 2 \\ \hline \end{array} \qquad \begin{array}{r} 2 \\ \times\ 2 \\ \hline \end{array} \qquad \begin{array}{r} 5 \\ \times\ 2 \\ \hline \end{array} \qquad \begin{array}{r} 0 \\ \times\ 2 \\ \hline \end{array}$$

$$\begin{array}{r} 2 \\ \times\ 2 \\ \hline \end{array} \qquad \begin{array}{r} 2 \\ \times\ 8 \\ \hline \end{array} \qquad \begin{array}{r} 2 \\ \times\ 1 \\ \hline \end{array} \qquad \begin{array}{r} 2 \\ \times\ 7 \\ \hline \end{array} \qquad \begin{array}{r} 2 \\ \times\ 5 \\ \hline \end{array}$$

$$\begin{array}{r} 2 \\ \times\ 0 \\ \hline \end{array} \qquad \begin{array}{r} 2 \\ \times\ 4 \\ \hline \end{array} \qquad \begin{array}{r} 2 \\ \times\ 6 \\ \hline \end{array} \qquad \begin{array}{r} 2 \\ \times\ 3 \\ \hline \end{array} \qquad \begin{array}{r} 2 \\ \times\ 9 \\ \hline \end{array}$$

$$\begin{array}{r} 5 \\ \times\ 2 \\ \hline \end{array} \qquad \begin{array}{r} 2 \\ \times\ 8 \\ \hline \end{array} \qquad \begin{array}{r} 6 \\ \times\ 2 \\ \hline \end{array} \qquad \begin{array}{r} 2 \\ \times\ 4 \\ \hline \end{array} \qquad \begin{array}{r} 1 \\ \times\ 2 \\ \hline \end{array}$$

Score: _____

Name ● **LESSON 117A**
(Draw a 4-inch line segment.)   **Math 2**

Date ●————————●
(Measure this line segment using inches. _____ inches)

1. The children were walking in pairs. George counted eight pairs of children. Draw X's to show the children.

How many children is that? _____

2. How much money is this? Write the amount two ways. _____ _____

_____ "

3. Measure the sides of the rectangle in Problem 2 using inches. What is the perimeter?

Number sentence _____ Answer _____

4. Find an example of parallel lines in the classroom.

What did you find? _____

5. Show 6:45 on the clockface.

6. Draw a line of symmetry in each shape. Color one half of each shape.

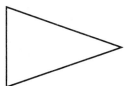   

7. Find the answers.

$4 + 6 + 2 + 9 + 3 + 8 + 4 + 7 + 1$ $83 - 75$ $63 + 21 + 34$

1. The children were playing in pairs. Linda counted four pairs of children. Draw X's to show the children.

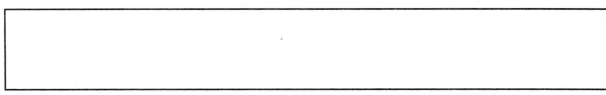

   How many children is that? _____

2. How much money is this? Write the amount two ways. _____ _____

   15 cm

   3 cm

3. Someone measured the sides of the rectangle in Problem 2. What is the perimeter?

   Number sentence _____

   Answer _____

4. Find an example of parallel lines at home.

   What did you find? _____

5. Show 10:15 on the clockface.

6. Draw a line of symmetry in each shape. Color one half of each shape.

7. Find the answers.

   6 + 2 + 4 + 5 + 9 + 8 + 1   73 − 56   24 + 37 + 23

11	10	6	9	12
− 9	− 4	− 2	− 5	− 3

16	7	14	12	11
− 9	− 3	− 5	− 6	− 6

10	15	5	13	8
− 7	− 8	− 2	− 7	− 6

12	5	11	9	16
− 3	− 0	− 5	− 2	− 7

15	8	15	9	7
− 9	− 1	− 7	− 9	− 4

Score: _____

Name _____ •

(Draw a 10 cm line segment.)

Date _____ •————————————————————————•

(Measure this line segment using centimeters. _____ cm)

1. Quinton has 9 baseball cards. Curtis has twice as many baseball cards as Quinton.

   How many baseball cards does Curtis have? _____

2. There are five children in line. Draw the children. You are fourth. Circle yourself.

   How many children are before you? _____

   How many children are after you? _____

   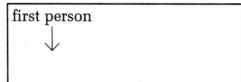

3. Each number is between what two tens?

   _____ , 17, _____   _____ , 43, _____   _____ , 35, _____

   Circle the 10 each number would be rounded to.

4. Gina has 2 quarters, 3 dimes, 2 nickels, and a penny. Draw the coins. How much money does she have?

   Write the answer two different ways. _____   _____

5. Fill in the missing numbers in the number patterns.

   80, 85, 90, _____ , _____ , _____ , _____ , _____ , _____

   _____ , _____ , _____ , 46, 56, 66, _____ , _____ , _____

6. Find the answers.

   6 × 2 = _____   8 × 2 = _____   4 × 5 = _____

   18 + 6 + 52 = _____   63 − 49 = _____   38 + 42 = _____

Name _____

Date _____

1. Ariana has 7 stuffed animals. Her sister has twice as many stuffed animals.

   How many stuffed animals does Ariana's sister have? _____

2. There are six children in line. Draw the children. You are third. Circle yourself.

   How many children are before you? _____

   How many children are after you? _____

   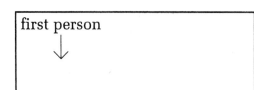

3. Each number is between what two tens?

   _____ , 24, _____   _____ , 58, _____   _____ , 25, _____

   Circle the 10 each number would be rounded to.

4. Daniel has 1 quarter, 2 dimes, 4 nickels, and 2 pennies. Draw the coins. How much money does he have?

   Write the answer two different ways. _____   _____

5. Fill in the missing numbers in the number patterns.

   92, 94, 96, _____ , _____ , _____ , _____ , _____ , _____

   _____ , _____ , _____ , 47, 57, 67, _____ , _____ , _____

6. Find the answers.

   7 × 2 = ____   9 × 2 = ____   6 × 5 = ____

   16 + 5 + 54 = ____   72 − 48 = ____   49 + 31 = ____

1.

____ groups of ____ wheels is ____ wheels

____ × ____ wheels = ____ wheels

2.

____ groups of ____ buttons is ____ buttons

____ × ____ buttons = ____ buttons

3.

____ groups of ____ raisins is ____ raisins

____ × ____ raisins = ____ raisins

4.

____ groups of ____ wheels is ____ wheels

____ × ____ wheels = ____ wheels

5.

_____ groups of _____ cookies is _____ cookies

_____ × _____ cookies = _____ cookies

6.

_____ × _____ = _____

7.

_____ × _____ = _____

8.

_____ × _____ = _____

12 − 4	8 − 3	9 − 6	11 − 8	12 − 5
14 − 6	11 − 4	13 − 5	12 − 8	9 − 3
11 − 7	13 − 8	12 − 7	8 − 5	14 − 8
11 − 3	9 − 6	12 − 4	13 − 5	11 − 8
14 − 6	8 − 3	11 − 4	12 − 8	12 − 5

Score: _____

Name •
(Draw a $4\frac{1}{2}''$ line segment.)

Date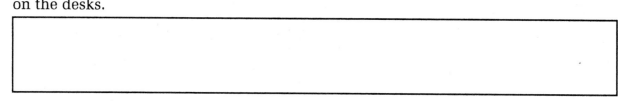
(Measure this line segment using inches. _____ ")

1. There are five desks in the room. T.J. put three books on each desk. Draw the books on the desks.

How many books did you draw altogether? _____

2. Round each number to the nearest 10.

    27 _____   52 _____   45 _____

3. Measure the vertical line segment on the left using centimeters.   _____cm

   Measure the vertical line segment on the right using centimeters.   _____cm

   Measure the horizontal line segment using centimeters.   _____cm

   Measure the oblique line segment using centimeters.   _____cm

   What is the perimeter of the shape?   _____cm

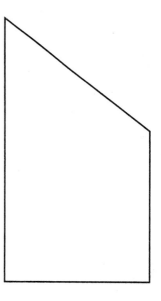

4. Trace the parallel line segments in Problem 3 using a red crayon.

5. Find an example of a cylinder in the classroom. What did you find? _____

   Find an example of a sphere in the classroom. What did you find? _____

6. Write six hundred seventeen using digits. _____

   Write this number in expanded form. _____

7. Find the answers.

   $9 \times 5 =$ _____ $7 \times 2 =$ _____

   $7 \times 10 =$ _____ $8 \times 100 =$ _____

$$\begin{array}{r} 4\ 5 \\ +\ 2\ 6 \\ \hline \end{array} \qquad \begin{array}{r} 7\ 1 \\ -\ 5\ 3 \\ \hline \end{array} \qquad \begin{array}{r} 8\ 5 \\ -\ 3\ 2 \\ \hline \end{array}$$

Name _____

Date _____

1. There are two tables in the room. Brenden put six books on each table. Draw the books on the tables.

    ┌───┐
    │   │
    │   │
    │   │
    └───┘

    How many books did you draw altogether? _____

2. Round each number to the nearest 10.

    19 _____   63 _____   75 _____

3. How long is the vertical line segment on the right? ____cm

    How long is the vertical line segment on the left? _____cm

    How long is the oblique line segment? _____cm

    How long is the horizontal line segment? _____cm

    What is the perimeter of the shape? _____cm

    5 cm

    8 cm

    4 cm

    3 cm

4. Trace the parallel line segments in Problem 3 using a red crayon.

5. Find an example of a cylinder at home. What did you find? _____

    Find an example of a sphere at home. What did you find? _____

6. Write two hundred thirty-seven using digits. _____

    Write this number in expanded form. _____

7. Find the answers.

    $3 \times 5 =$ _____ $6 \times 2 =$ _____

    $4 \times 10 =$ _____ $5 \times 100 =$ _____

    $$\begin{array}{r} 7\ 1 \\ +\ 6\ 9 \\ \hline \end{array} \qquad \begin{array}{r} 2\ 4 \\ -\ 1\ 6 \\ \hline \end{array} \qquad \begin{array}{r} 5\ 8 \\ -\ 1\ 7 \\ \hline \end{array}$$

Name _____

Date _____

1. Joshua had 42 baseball cards. He gave 15 cards to Dana. How many cards does he have now?

   Number sentence _____ Answer _____

2. Measure these line segments using centimeters.

    _____cm

   _____ _____cm

   Draw an 8 cm line segment.

   •

3. Show half past eleven on the clocks.

   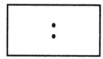

   What time is shown on this clock?

   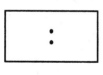

4. Use the correct comparison symbol (>, <, or =).

   6 + 3 ☐ 2 × 5   16 − 7 ☐ 10   27 + 23 ☐ 5 × 10

5. Find the answers.

   45 + 87 = _____

   4 8   5 1   5 9
   − 1 7   − 1 6   3 7
                          + 9 3

Name _____

Question _____

_____

Choices   1) _____

            2) _____

            3) _____

            4) _____

The title of the graph will be:

_____

<table>
<tr><th>Choices</th><th>Tally of votes</th></tr>
</table>

Choices   Tally of votes

1) _____   [ ]

2) _____   [ ]

3) _____   [ ]

4) _____   [ ]

If any choice receives more than 7 votes, number your graph by 2's.

Name _____

Title _____

_____ _____ _____ _____

Class surveyed: Grade _____ **Teacher** _____

6 × 2	1 × 2	9 × 2	4 × 2	7 × 2
3 × 2	8 × 2	2 × 2	5 × 2	0 × 2
2 × 2	2 × 8	2 × 1	2 × 7	2 × 5
2 × 0	2 × 4	2 × 6	2 × 3	2 × 9
5 × 2	2 × 8	6 × 2	2 × 4	1 × 2

Score: _____

2-120Fa

A.

B.

C.

5 + 4	4 + 6	2 + 3	6 + 8	5 + 0	0 + 9	4 + 8	5 + 6	1 + 3	6 + 1
2 + 5	0 + 8	6 + 7	0 + 3	2 + 9	8 + 8	6 + 0	1 + 9	6 + 9	8 + 4
1 + 6	9 + 8	1 + 5	4 + 9	8 + 6	2 + 4	7 + 9	8 + 3	4 + 3	0 + 4
7 + 3	3 + 2	7 + 0	7 + 2	1 + 4	6 + 5	3 + 6	3 + 0	8 + 0	9 + 7
9 + 9	7 + 8	7 + 4	9 + 5	5 + 7	1 + 8	0 + 1	8 + 9	2 + 7	7 + 5
0 + 7	6 + 6	3 + 3	2 + 6	6 + 2	9 + 2	5 + 8	4 + 5	9 + 3	3 + 1
5 + 1	4 + 1	8 + 1	3 + 4	0 + 0	4 + 4	9 + 6	1 + 2	5 + 9	2 + 8
6 + 4	8 + 7	0 + 6	7 + 6	1 + 7	3 + 7	9 + 0	4 + 7	0 + 2	5 + 3
2 + 2	2 + 0	3 + 9	5 + 5	3 + 5	0 + 5	7 + 7	2 + 6	3 + 8	4 + 0
9 + 1	9 + 4	5 + 2	1 + 0	8 + 2	6 + 3	4 + 2	7 + 1	1 + 1	8 + 5

Name
(Draw an 8 cm line segment.)

Date
(Measure the line segment using centimeters. _____ cm)

1. Dina told the class that she put two quarters in each of her pockets. Dina's clothing has 5 pockets. Draw the pockets. Draw the quarters in each pocket.

    How many quarters does she have? _____

    How much money is this? _____

2. Write the fraction that tells how much is shaded. _____

    Write the fraction that tells how much is not shaded. _____

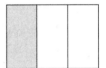

3. Show half past seven on the clocks.

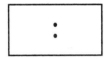

4. Round these numbers to the nearest 10.

    47 _____   12 _____   85 _____

5. Label these arrays.

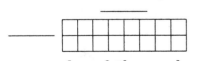

    number of tiles used _____

    _____ by _____ array

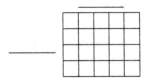

    number of tiles used _____

    _____ by _____ array

6. Find the answers.

    $41 + 19 =$ _____ $71 - 7 =$ _____ $52 - 39 =$ _____

1. Millie told the class that she put five dimes in each of her pockets. Millie's clothing has 3 pockets. Draw the pockets. Draw the dimes in each pocket.

   How many dimes does she have? _____

   How much money is this? _____

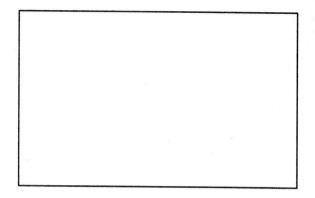

2. Write the fraction that tells how much is shaded. _____

   Write the fraction that tells how much is not shaded. _____

3. Show half past two on the clocks.

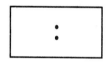

4. Round these numbers to the nearest 10.

   66 _____   8 _____   75 _____

5. Label these arrays.

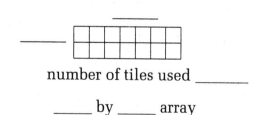

   number of tiles used _____

   _____ by _____ array

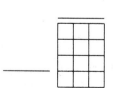

   number of tiles used _____

   _____ by _____ array

6. Find the answers.

   $28 + 62 =$ _____ $42 - 6 =$ _____ $71 - 58 =$ _____

Shapes With Right Angles

1.

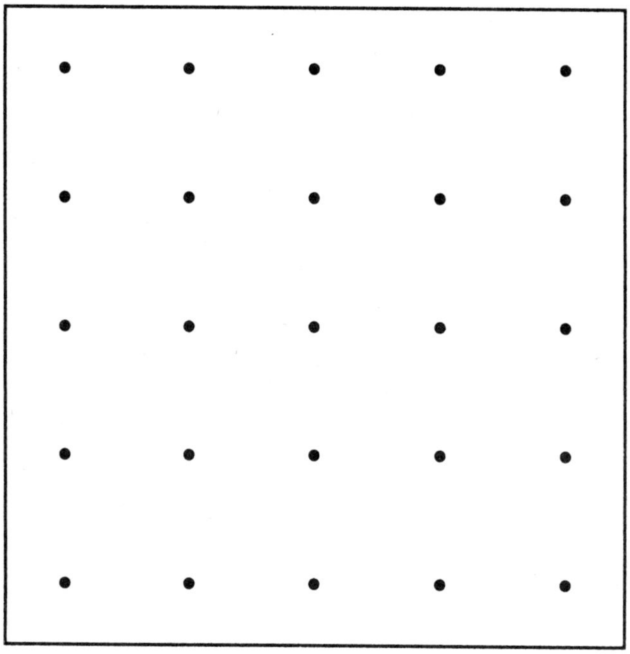

2.

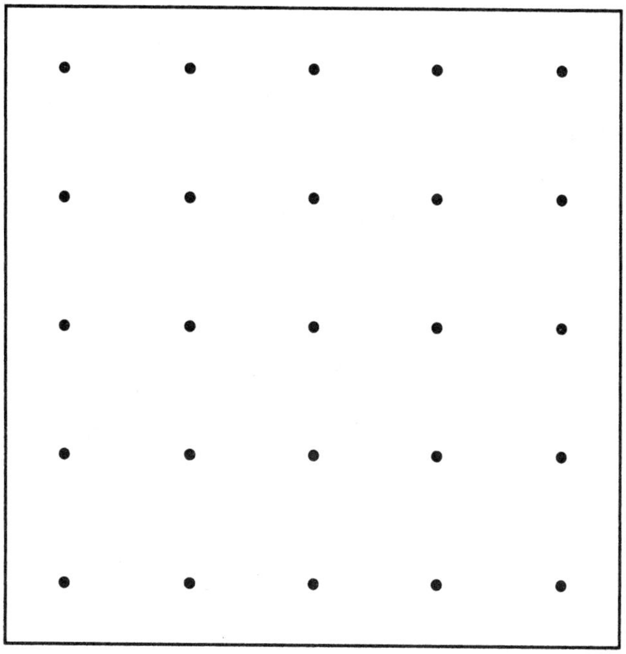

3.

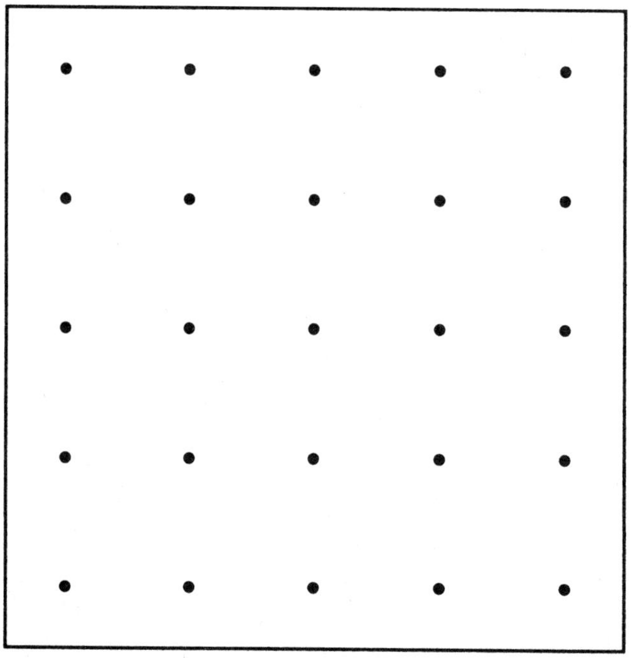

4.

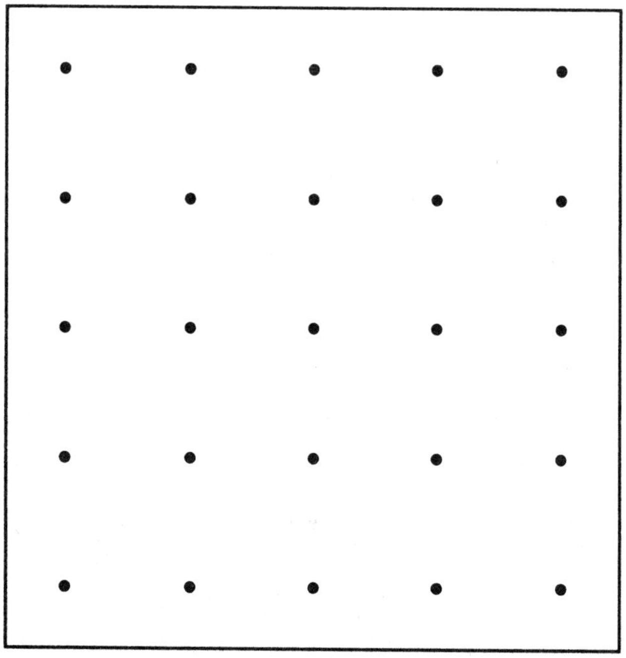

$$
\begin{array}{r} 4 \\ \times\ 5 \\ \hline \end{array}
\qquad
\begin{array}{r} 2 \\ \times\ 6 \\ \hline \end{array}
\qquad
\begin{array}{r} 5 \\ \times\ 7 \\ \hline \end{array}
\qquad
\begin{array}{r} 6 \\ \times\ 10 \\ \hline \end{array}
\qquad
\begin{array}{r} 9 \\ \times\ 2 \\ \hline \end{array}
$$

$$
\begin{array}{r} 6 \\ \times\ 5 \\ \hline \end{array}
\qquad
\begin{array}{r} 10 \\ \times\ 9 \\ \hline \end{array}
\qquad
\begin{array}{r} 6 \\ \times\ 2 \\ \hline \end{array}
\qquad
\begin{array}{r} 2 \\ \times\ 4 \\ \hline \end{array}
\qquad
\begin{array}{r} 3 \\ \times\ 5 \\ \hline \end{array}
$$

$$
\begin{array}{r} 2 \\ \times\ 10 \\ \hline \end{array}
\qquad
\begin{array}{r} 2 \\ \times\ 7 \\ \hline \end{array}
\qquad
\begin{array}{r} 5 \\ \times\ 9 \\ \hline \end{array}
\qquad
\begin{array}{r} 10 \\ \times\ 8 \\ \hline \end{array}
\qquad
\begin{array}{r} 5 \\ \times\ 2 \\ \hline \end{array}
$$

$$
\begin{array}{r} 3 \\ \times\ 10 \\ \hline \end{array}
\qquad
\begin{array}{r} 5 \\ \times\ 5 \\ \hline \end{array}
\qquad
\begin{array}{r} 2 \\ \times\ 8 \\ \hline \end{array}
\qquad
\begin{array}{r} 5 \\ \times\ 1 \\ \hline \end{array}
\qquad
\begin{array}{r} 10 \\ \times\ 10 \\ \hline \end{array}
$$

$$
\begin{array}{r} 3 \\ \times\ 2 \\ \hline \end{array}
\qquad
\begin{array}{r} 0 \\ \times\ 5 \\ \hline \end{array}
\qquad
\begin{array}{r} 10 \\ \times\ 5 \\ \hline \end{array}
\qquad
\begin{array}{r} 8 \\ \times\ 10 \\ \hline \end{array}
\qquad
\begin{array}{r} 8 \\ \times\ 5 \\ \hline \end{array}
$$

Score: _____

Name _____ •

(Draw a 12 cm line segment.)

Date •————————————————•

(Measure the line segment using centimeters. _____ cm)

1. The children in Mrs. Ammerman's class chose their favorite fruits. Eight children chose bananas, fifteen children chose oranges, and seven children chose apples. Shade the graph to show how many children chose each type of fruit.

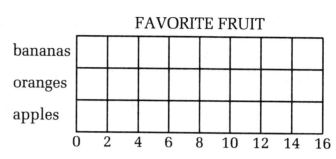

FAVORITE FRUIT

bananas

oranges

apples

0 2 4 6 8 10 12 14 16

Write your observations about this graph. _____

_____

_____

2. Put a small square in each right angle of this shape.
(Use a corner of a piece of paper to check the angle.)

How many right angles are there? _____

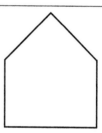

3. Trace the parallel line segments in Problem 2 using a red crayon.

4. I had 5 dimes and 14 pennies. I traded pennies for a dime.

How many dimes and pennies do I have now? _____ dimes _____ pennies

5. Draw 3 baskets. Draw 4 oranges in each basket.

How many oranges did you draw? _____

6. Circle the name of this array.

3 + 6   3 by 6   15 + 3   6 by 6

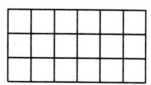

7. Find the answers.

$9 \times 5 =$ ____ $68 - 39 =$ ____

$8 \times 2 =$ ____ $58 + 37 + 25 =$ ____

2-122Wa

1. The children in Mrs. Albright's class chose their favorite fruits. Six children chose bananas, thirteen children chose oranges, and nine children chose apples. Shade the graph to show how many children chose each type of fruit.

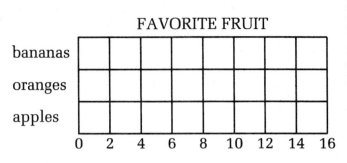

Write your observations about this graph. _____

_____

_____

2. Put a small square in each right angle of this shape. (Use a corner of a piece of paper to check the angle.)

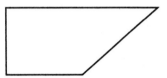

How many right angles are there? _____

3. Trace the parallel line segments in Problem 2 using a red crayon.

4. I had 4 dimes and 17 pennies. I traded pennies for a dime.

How many dimes and pennies do I have now? _____ dimes _____ pennies

5. Draw 4 baskets. Draw 3 apples in each basket.

How many apples did you draw? _____

6. Circle the name of this array.

5 by 5   8 + 2   2 by 5   5 + 2

7. Find the answers.

$7 \times 5 =$ _____ $94 - 58 =$ _____

$9 \times 2 =$ _____ $77 + 35 + 81 =$ _____

7 − 1	10 − 4	9 − 0	16 − 9	5 − 4	12 − 6	9 − 7	11 − 3	8 − 2	6 − 6
9 − 4	6 − 3	11 − 6	10 − 2	6 − 1	12 − 8	2 − 0	9 − 3	7 − 2	6 − 5
5 − 5	11 − 4	4 − 2	15 − 9	8 − 0	10 − 6	14 − 5	9 − 9	7 − 6	12 − 7
9 − 5	17 − 9	8 − 4	13 − 8	9 − 2	11 − 5	15 − 6	5 − 1	8 − 5	16 − 8
8 − 6	11 − 7	1 − 0	7 − 3	9 − 6	4 − 3	17 − 8	10 − 5	12 − 4	13 − 7
8 − 3	16 − 7	10 − 3	4 − 1	6 − 2	13 − 5	7 − 0	14 − 9	11 − 2	10 − 8
13 − 9	10 − 7	18 − 9	14 − 6	1 − 1	12 − 3	7 − 5	4 − 1	11 − 8	7 − 7
2 − 2	12 − 5	3 − 1	15 − 7	10 − 1	6 − 0	13 − 4	5 − 2	9 − 8	3 − 0
11 − 9	7 − 6	13 − 6	3 − 3	14 − 8	9 − 1	6 − 4	12 − 9	7 − 4	8 − 7
4 − 4	15 − 8	3 − 2	5 − 0	5 − 3	8 − 8	14 − 7	10 − 9	0 − 0	8 − 1

Name ●
(Draw a 9 cm line segment.)

Date ●————————————————————————————————————●
(Measure the line segment using centimeters. _____ cm)

1. There were 6 children at the party. Aunt Angie put 5 strawberries on each child's dish of ice cream.

   What type of story is this? _____
   Draw a picture to show the strawberries on the dishes of ice cream.

   ┌───┐
   │   │
   │   │
   │   │
   └───┘

   How many strawberries did Aunt Angie use altogether?

   Number sentence _____ Answer _____

2. How much money is this?
   Write the amount two
   ways.

   _____ _____

3. Measure the sides of the rectangle in Problem 2 using centimeters. What is the perimeter?

   Number sentence _____

   Answer _____

4. Draw a triangle with a right angle.

5. Label this array.

   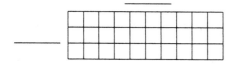

       number of tiles used _____

       _____ by _____ array

   ┌─────────────────────────────────┐
   │   │
   │   │
   │   │
   │   │
   └─────────────────────────────────┘

6. Write two hundred seven using digits. _____

   Write two hundred seven in expanded form. _____

7. Find the answers.

       7 × 2 = _____   8 × 5 = _____   9 × 100 = _____

2-123Wa

1. There were 8 children. Miss Natiello put 2 stickers on each child's paper.

    What type of story is this? _____
    Draw a picture to show the stickers on the papers.

    ┌───┐
    │   │
    │   │
    │   │
    │   │
    └───┘

    How many stickers did Miss Natiello use altogether?

    Number sentence _____ Answer _____

2. How much money is this? Write the amount two ways. _____ _____

    11 cm

    3 cm  3 cm

    11 cm

3. Find the perimeter of the rectangle in Problem 2.

    Number sentence _____

    Answer _____

4. Draw a shape with 4 right angles.

    ┌─────────────────────────────────────┐
    │   │
    │   │
    │   │
    │   │
    │   │
    └─────────────────────────────────────┘

5. Label this array.   _____

    _____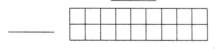

    number of tiles used _____

    _____ by _____ array

6. Write four hundred sixteen using digits. _____

    Write four hundred sixteen in expanded form. _____

7. Find the answers.

    $3 \times 5 =$ _____ $9 \times 2 =$ _____ $4 \times 100 =$ _____

$$\begin{array}{r} 2 \\ \times\ 3 \\ \hline \end{array} \qquad \begin{array}{r} 7 \\ \times\ 3 \\ \hline \end{array} \qquad \begin{array}{r} 1 \\ \times\ 3 \\ \hline \end{array} \qquad \begin{array}{r} 3 \\ \times\ 5 \\ \hline \end{array} \qquad \begin{array}{r} 4 \\ \times\ 3 \\ \hline \end{array}$$

$$\begin{array}{r} 6 \\ \times\ 3 \\ \hline \end{array} \qquad \begin{array}{r} 3 \\ \times\ 8 \\ \hline \end{array} \qquad \begin{array}{r} 3 \\ \times\ 4 \\ \hline \end{array} \qquad \begin{array}{r} 9 \\ \times\ 3 \\ \hline \end{array} \qquad \begin{array}{r} 3 \\ \times\ 3 \\ \hline \end{array}$$

$$\begin{array}{r} 3 \\ \times\ 0 \\ \hline \end{array} \qquad \begin{array}{r} 8 \\ \times\ 3 \\ \hline \end{array} \qquad \begin{array}{r} 3 \\ \times\ 5 \\ \hline \end{array} \qquad \begin{array}{r} 9 \\ \times\ 3 \\ \hline \end{array} \qquad \begin{array}{r} 3 \\ \times\ 6 \\ \hline \end{array}$$

$$\begin{array}{r} 8 \\ \times\ 3 \\ \hline \end{array} \qquad \begin{array}{r} 3 \\ \times\ 2 \\ \hline \end{array} \qquad \begin{array}{r} 3 \\ \times\ 4 \\ \hline \end{array} \qquad \begin{array}{r} 6 \\ \times\ 3 \\ \hline \end{array} \qquad \begin{array}{r} 0 \\ \times\ 3 \\ \hline \end{array}$$

$$\begin{array}{r} 3 \\ \times\ 7 \\ \hline \end{array} \qquad \begin{array}{r} 1 \\ \times\ 3 \\ \hline \end{array} \qquad \begin{array}{r} 6 \\ \times\ 3 \\ \hline \end{array} \qquad \begin{array}{r} 3 \\ \times\ 7 \\ \hline \end{array} \qquad \begin{array}{r} 3 \\ \times\ 3 \\ \hline \end{array}$$

Score: _____

Name

(Draw a 12 cm line segment.)

Date

(Measure the line segment using centimeters. _____ cm)

1. Pencils are sold in packages of 3. Mrs. Doster bought 7 packages of pencils.

   What type of story is this? _____

   Draw a picture to show the packages of pencils.

   How many pencils did she buy?

   Number sentence _____ Answer _____

2. Write the fraction that tells how much is shaded. _____

   Write the fraction that tells how much is not shaded. _____

3. Davina has 4 quarters, a nickel, and 7 pennies. Draw the coins.

   How much money is this? _____

4. Find the answers.

$$
\begin{array}{cccccccccc}
3 & 3 & 3 & 3 & 3 & 3 & 3 & 3 & 3 & 3 & 3 \\
\times\,7 & \times\,3 & \times\,9 & \times\,1 & \times\,4 & \times\,10 & \times\,2 & \times\,6 & \times\,8 & \times\,0 & \times\,5
\end{array}
$$

5. Draw a small square to show the right angle.

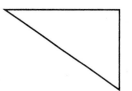

6. Find the answers.

$$
\begin{array}{ccc}
5\,8 & 8\,5 & 9\,4 \\
-\,3\,4 & +\,3\,5 & -\,2\,5
\end{array}
$$

$6 + 2 + 3 + 7 + 9 + 1 = $ _____

1. Pencils are sold in packages of 10. Mrs. Campion bought 9 packages.

   What type of story is this? _____

   Draw a picture to show the packages of pencils.

   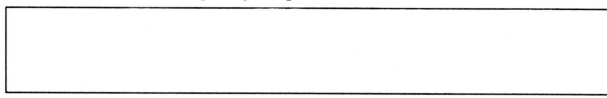

   How many pencils did she buy?

   Number sentence _____ Answer _____

2. Write the fraction that tells how much is shaded. _____

   Write the fraction that tells how much is not shaded. _____

3. Karen has 5 quarters, a nickel, and 2 pennies. Draw the coins.

   How much money is this? _____

   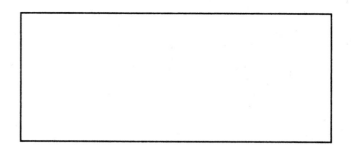

4. Fill in the missing numbers.

   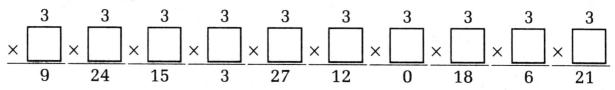

5. Draw a small square to show the right angle.

   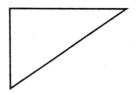

6. Find the answers.

   $$\begin{array}{r} 8\;5 \\ -\;4\;3 \\ \hline \end{array} \qquad \begin{array}{r} 9\;1 \\ +\;4\;7 \\ \hline \end{array} \qquad \begin{array}{r} 6\;2 \\ -\;5\;7 \\ \hline \end{array}$$

   $7 + 3 + 2 + 9 + 8 + 4 + 1 =$ _____

1. There are 4 children in Paul's group. Each child has 5 markers. Draw the markers.

   How many markers do the children in Paul's group have altogether? _____

2. Measure the length of each side of this shape using centimeters.

   What is the perimeter? _____

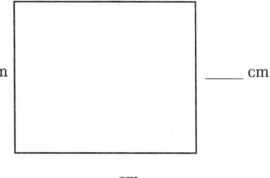

   _____ cm

   _____ cm   _____ cm

   _____ cm

3. Use a crayon to trace an example of parallel lines on this paper.

   Where do you see parallel lines in the classroom?

   _____

4. I have 1 quarter, 4 dimes, 1 nickel, and 2 pennies. Draw the coins. How much money do I have?

   Write the amount two ways.

   _____   _____

5. Find the answers.

   $6 \times 2 =$ _____ $8 \times 10 =$ _____

   $3 \times 5 =$ _____ $9 \times 2 =$ _____

   $$\begin{array}{r} 4\ 5 \\ -\ 2\ 9 \\ \hline \end{array}$$

   $$\begin{array}{r} 7\ 0 \\ -\ 3\ 4 \\ \hline \end{array}$$

   $$\begin{array}{r} 3\ 8 \\ 4\ 7 \\ +\ 6\ 5 \\ \hline \end{array}$$

Perpendicular Line Segments

1.

2.

3.

4.

2 × 3	7 × 3	1 × 3	3 × 5	4 × 3
6 × 3	3 × 8	3 × 4	9 × 3	3 × 3
3 × 0	8 × 3	3 × 5	9 × 3	3 × 6
8 × 3	3 × 2	3 × 4	6 × 3	0 × 3
3 × 7	1 × 3	6 × 3	3 × 7	3 × 3

Score: _____

Name ●

(Draw a 3" line segment.)

Date ●————————————————————————●

(Measure this line segment using inches. _____ ")

1. Twenty-six children were in the gym. Seventeen children from another class joined them.

   What type of story is this? _____

   How many children are in the gym now?

   Number sentence _____ Answer _____

2. Circle the perpendicular line segments.

3. About how much might a 7-year-old child weigh?

   200 pounds   60 pounds   15 pounds   2 pounds

4. Round each number to the nearest 10.

   78 _____   13 _____   25 _____

5. Circle all the geometric solids that have at least one point.

   pyramid   cylinder   cone   sphere   cube

6. Find the answers.

$$
\begin{array}{rr}
& 6\ 8 \\
6\ 2 & 3\ 7 \\
-\ 3\ 8 & +\ 2\ 5 \\
\hline
\end{array}
$$

   $2 \times 3 =$ _____ $8 \times 10 =$ _____

   $7 \times 3 =$ _____ $3 \times 100 =$ _____

   $9 \times 3 =$ _____ $5 \times 3 =$ _____

1. There were forty-three children in the gym. Fifteen children went back to class.

   What type of story is this? _____

   How many children are in the gym now?

   Number sentence _____ Answer _____

2. Circle the perpendicular line segments.

3. About how much might a 10-year-old child weigh?

   25 pounds   300 pounds   90 pounds   4 pounds

4. Round each number to the nearest 10.

   31 _____   9 _____   15 _____

5. Circle all the geometric solids that will roll.

   pyramid   cylinder   cone   sphere

6. Find the answers.

   $$\begin{array}{r} 7\,1 \\ -\,2\,5 \\ \hline \end{array}$$
   $$\begin{array}{r} 7\,9 \\ 2\,6 \\ +\,3\,5 \\ \hline \end{array}$$

   4 × 3 = _____   7 × 10 = _____

   6 × 3 = _____   2 × 100 = _____

   3 × 3 = _____   8 × 3 = _____

4 × 5	2 × 6	5 × 7	6 × 10	9 × 2
6 × 5	10 × 9	6 × 2	2 × 4	3 × 5
2 × 10	2 × 7	5 × 9	10 × 8	5 × 2
3 × 10	5 × 5	2 × 8	5 × 1	10 × 10
3 × 2	0 × 5	10 × 5	8 × 10	8 × 5

Score: _____

Name _____ •

(Draw a 2½" line segment.)

Date •————————————•

(Measure this line segment using inches. _____ ")

1. Three children can sit at each table in Room 7. There are ten tables in the room. Draw a picture to show the tables and chairs in Room 7.

How many children can sit in Room 7?

Number sentence _____ Answer _____

2. Find an example of perpendicular line segments on this paper. Trace them with a crayon.

3. Round each number to the nearest 10 and add the rounded numbers.

   63 + 29   31 + 48

   _____ + _____ = _____   _____ + _____ = _____

4. Label this array. Write a number sentence for the array.

   _____

   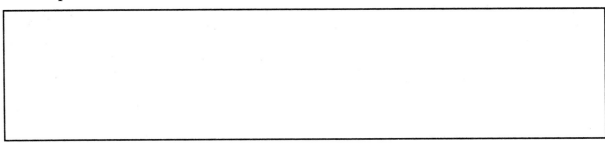

5. Use the correct comparison symbol (>, <, or =).

   35 ☐ 53   8 + 42 ☐ 5 × 10   16 − 7 ☐ 14 − 6

6. Find the answers.

   59 + 87 = _____   74 − 28 = _____   7 + 63 + 51 = _____

1. Mrs. Wagoner has 5 games for the children to use during recess. Four children can play each game. Draw a picture to show the games and children.

   [box]

   How many children can play the games?

   Number sentence _____ Answer _____

2. Find an example of perpendicular line segments on this paper. Trace them with a crayon.

3. Round each number to the nearest 10 and add the rounded numbers.

   28 + 49   52 + 39

   _____ + _____ = _____   _____ + _____ = _____

4. Label this array. Write a number sentence for the array.

   _____

5. Use the correct comparison symbol (>, <, or =).

   68 ☐ 86   3 + 27 ☐ 5 × 6   17 − 9 ☐ 13 − 4

6. Find the answers.

   65 + 86 = _____   85 − 27 = _____   59 + 61 + 8 = _____

7 − 1	10 − 4	9 − 0	16 − 9	5 − 4	12 − 6	9 − 7	11 − 3	8 − 2	6 − 6
9 − 4	6 − 3	11 − 6	10 − 2	6 − 1	12 − 8	2 − 0	9 − 3	7 − 2	6 − 5
5 − 5	11 − 4	4 − 2	15 − 9	8 − 0	10 − 6	14 − 5	9 − 9	7 − 6	12 − 7
9 − 5	17 − 9	8 − 4	13 − 8	9 − 2	11 − 5	15 − 6	5 − 1	8 − 5	16 − 8
8 − 6	11 − 7	1 − 0	7 − 3	9 − 6	4 − 3	17 − 8	10 − 5	12 − 4	13 − 7
8 − 3	16 − 7	10 − 3	4 − 1	6 − 2	13 − 5	7 − 0	14 − 9	11 − 2	10 − 8
13 − 9	10 − 7	18 − 9	14 − 6	1 − 1	12 − 3	7 − 5	4 − 1	11 − 8	7 − 7
2 − 2	12 − 5	3 − 1	15 − 7	10 − 1	6 − 0	13 − 4	5 − 2	9 − 8	3 − 0
11 − 9	7 − 6	13 − 6	3 − 3	14 − 8	9 − 1	6 − 4	12 − 9	7 − 4	8 − 7
4 − 4	15 − 8	3 − 2	5 − 0	5 − 3	8 − 8	14 − 7	10 − 9	0 − 0	8 − 1

Name _____

(Draw an 11 cm line segment.)

Date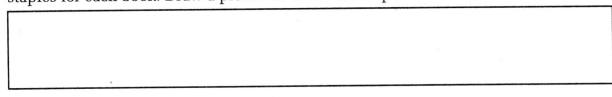

(Measure the line segment using inches. _____ " Write the date using digits.)

1. Nine children in Mrs. O'Neill's class assembled books. The children used three staples for each book. Draw a picture to show the staples in the books.

How many staples did they use for the books?

Number sentence _____ Answer _____

2. Write number sentences for these arrays.

_____   _____

3. Measure each side of this shape using centimeters.

   How long is the vertical line segment? _____

   How long is the oblique line segment? _____

   How long is the horizontal line segment? _____

   What is the perimeter? _____

4. Trace the perpendicular line segments in Problem 3 using a crayon.

5. I have 2 quarters, 2 dimes, 3 nickels, and 7 pennies. Draw the coins.

   How much money do I have? _____

6. Find the answers.

   63 + 94 = _____   94 − 77 = _____

1. Four children in Mrs. Sheehan's class made picture books. Each book had 10 pictures. Draw a picture to show the pictures in the books.

   How many pictures are in the books?

   Number sentence _____ Answer _____

2. Write number sentences for these arrays.

   _____   _____

3. Someone measured each side of this shape using inches.

   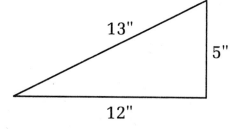

   How long is the vertical line segment? _____

   How long is the oblique line segment? _____

   How long is the horizontal line segment? _____

   What is the perimeter? _____

4. Trace the perpendicular line segments in Problem 3 using a crayon.

5. I have 1 quarter, 3 dimes, 1 nickel, and 9 pennies. Draw the coins.

   How much money do I have? _____

6. Find the answers.

   75 + 37 = _____   81 − 43 = _____

2	7	1	3	4
× 3	× 3	× 3	× 5	× 3

6	3	3	9	3
× 3	× 8	× 4	× 3	× 3

3	8	3	9	3
× 0	× 3	× 5	× 3	× 6

8	3	3	6	0
× 3	× 2	× 4	× 3	× 3

3	1	6	3	3
× 7	× 3	× 3	× 7	× 3

Score: _____

Name •
(Draw an 11 cm line segment.)

Date •————————•
(Measure this line segment using centimeters. _____ cm)

1. The children in Mrs. Cambias's class read 37 books, the children in Mrs. Roberts's class read 28 books, and the children in Mrs. Ambrose's class read 25 books. How many books did the children in the three classes read altogether?

   Number sentence _____ Answer _____

2. How can you check to see if a shape has a right angle?

   Draw an example of a right angle.

   _____ _____

   _____

3. Round each number to the nearest 10.

   13 _____   45 _____   76 _____

4. Put a red dot at (3, 0).

   Put a blue dot at (2, 4).

   ```
   4  •   •   •   •   •
   3  •   •   •   •   •
   2  •   •   •   •   •
   1  •   •   •   •   •
   0  •   •   •   •   •
      0   1   2   3   4
   ```

5. Write the full date for 3/14/95.

   _____

6. Find the answers.

   $5 \times 3 =$ _____ $6 \times 2 =$ _____ $9 \times 100 =$ _____

   $70 - 42 =$ _____ $63 - 18 =$ _____

   $$\begin{array}{r} 42 \\ 38 \\ +\ 17 \\ \hline \end{array} \qquad \begin{array}{r} 29 \\ 59 \\ +\ 32 \\ \hline \end{array}$$

Name _____   **LESSON 128B**

Date _____   *Math 2*

1. Craig has 36 markers, Eric has 24 markers, and Ryan has 48 markers. How many markers do the three boys have altogether?

   Number sentence _____ Answer _____

2. Use the corner of this piece of paper to find four examples of right angles at home. What did you find?

   _____   _____

   _____   _____

3. Round each number to the nearest 10.

   18 _____   74 _____   85 _____

4. Put a red dot at (3, 4).

   Put a blue dot at (1, 2).

   4 •   •   •   •   •

   3 •   •   •   •   •

   2 •   •   •   •   •

   1 •   •   •   •   •

5. Write the full date for 7/9/97.

   0 •   •   •   •   •

       0   1   2   3   4

   _____

6. Find the answers.

   $9 \times 3 =$ _____ $7 \times 2 =$ _____ $3 \times 100 =$ _____

   $18 + 54 =$ _____ $52 - 17 =$ _____

   $$\begin{array}{r} 3\ 8 \\ 5\ 2 \\ +\ 7\ 6 \\ \hline \end{array}$$ $$\begin{array}{r} 1\ 6 \\ 5\ 7 \\ +\ 6\ 2 \\ \hline \end{array}$$

$$\begin{array}{r} 4 \\ \times\ 4 \\ \hline \end{array} \qquad \begin{array}{r} 4 \\ \times\ 10 \\ \hline \end{array} \qquad \begin{array}{r} 1 \\ \times\ 4 \\ \hline \end{array} \qquad \begin{array}{r} 8 \\ \times\ 4 \\ \hline \end{array} \qquad \begin{array}{r} 4 \\ \times\ 3 \\ \hline \end{array}$$

$$\begin{array}{r} 4 \\ \times\ 5 \\ \hline \end{array} \qquad \begin{array}{r} 4 \\ \times\ 9 \\ \hline \end{array} \qquad \begin{array}{r} 6 \\ \times\ 4 \\ \hline \end{array} \qquad \begin{array}{r} 2 \\ \times\ 4 \\ \hline \end{array} \qquad \begin{array}{r} 4 \\ \times\ 7 \\ \hline \end{array}$$

$$\begin{array}{r} 0 \\ \times\ 4 \\ \hline \end{array} \qquad \begin{array}{r} 6 \\ \times\ 4 \\ \hline \end{array} \qquad \begin{array}{r} 4 \\ \times\ 4 \\ \hline \end{array} \qquad \begin{array}{r} 2 \\ \times\ 4 \\ \hline \end{array} \qquad \begin{array}{r} 4 \\ \times\ 9 \\ \hline \end{array}$$

$$\begin{array}{r} 4 \\ \times\ 7 \\ \hline \end{array} \qquad \begin{array}{r} 4 \\ \times\ 5 \\ \hline \end{array} \qquad \begin{array}{r} 4 \\ \times\ 1 \\ \hline \end{array} \qquad \begin{array}{r} 8 \\ \times\ 4 \\ \hline \end{array} \qquad \begin{array}{r} 3 \\ \times\ 4 \\ \hline \end{array}$$

$$\begin{array}{r} 4 \\ \times\ 10 \\ \hline \end{array} \qquad \begin{array}{r} 3 \\ \times\ 4 \\ \hline \end{array} \qquad \begin{array}{r} 4 \\ \times\ 5 \\ \hline \end{array} \qquad \begin{array}{r} 7 \\ \times\ 4 \\ \hline \end{array} \qquad \begin{array}{r} 4 \\ \times\ 0 \\ \hline \end{array}$$

Score: _____

Name •

(Draw an 8 cm line segment.)

Date •———————————————————————•

(Measure this line segment using centimeters. _____ cm)

1. The boys in Mrs. Topalanchik's class collected 74 buttons. The girls collected 17 buttons. The boys gave the girls 25 of their buttons. How many buttons do the boys have now?

   Number sentence _____ Answer _____

2. Write December 31, 1965 using digits. _____

3. Write a number sentence for this array.

   _____

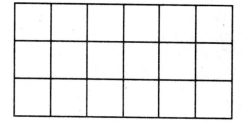

4. Measure the sides of the rectangle in Problem 3 using centimeters.

   What is the perimeter of the rectangle? _____

5. Color half of the small squares in Problem 3 red. Color the other half of the small squares in Problem 3 Yellow.

   How many squares are red? _____

   How many squares are yellow? _____

6. Put a red dot at (1, 3).
   Put a blue dot at (2, 0).

```
4  •   •   •   •   •

3  •   •   •   •   •

2  •   •   •   •   •

1  •   •   •   •   •

0  •   •   •   •   •

   0   1   2   3   4
```

7. Find the answers.

$$\begin{array}{cccccccccc} 4 & 4 & 4 & 4 & 4 & 4 & 4 & 4 & 4 & 4 \\ \times\,3 & \times\,6 & \times\,0 & \times\,9 & \times\,4 & \times\,1 & \times\,7 & \times\,5 & \times\,8 & \times\,2 \end{array}$$

Name _____

Date _____

1. Harvey collected 27 brown stones and 16 white stones. Andy collected 36 brown stones and 18 white stones. How many brown stones do the two boys have altogether?

    Number sentence _____ Answer _____

2. Write October 17, 1958 using digits. _____

3. Write a number sentence for
    this array.

    _____

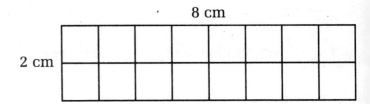

8 cm

2 cm

4. Someone measured the sides of the rectangle in Problem 3 using centimeters.

    What is the perimeter of the rectangle? _____

5. Color half of the small squares in Problem 3 red. Color the other half of the small squares in Problem 3 yellow.

    How many squares are red? _____

    How many squares are yellow? _____

    4 • • • • •

    3 • • • • •

    2 • • • • •

6. Put a red dot at (0, 4).
    Put a blue dot at (4, 3).

    1 • • • • •

    0 • • • • •

       0 1 2 3 4

7. Fill in the missing numbers.

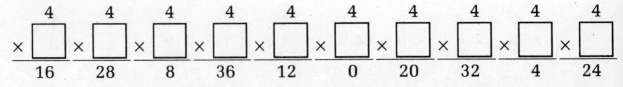

4	4	4	4	4	4	4	4	4	4
× ☐	× ☐	× ☐	× ☐	× ☐	× ☐	× ☐	× ☐	× ☐	× ☐
16	28	8	36	12	0	20	32	4	24

1. There are 5 tables in Room 7. There are 3 books on each table. Draw a picture of the books on the tables.

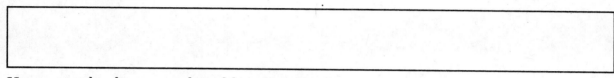

How many books are on the tables altogether?

Number sentence _____ Answer _____

2. Circle the shapes that have a right angle.

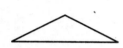  

3. Write a number sentence for this array.

_____

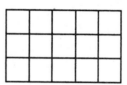

4. Round each number to the nearest 10.

23 _____   35 _____   87 _____

5. Use the graph to answer the question.

How many children have cats? _____

Write two facts about this graph.

_____

_____

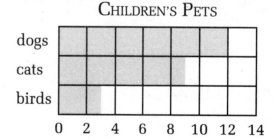

CHILDREN'S PETS

6. Find the answers.

$$\begin{array}{r} 7\ 9 \\ +\ 5\ 3 \\ \hline \end{array}$$
$$\begin{array}{r} 6\ 1 \\ -\ 2\ 5 \\ \hline \end{array}$$
16 + 54 = _____
84 − 57 = _____

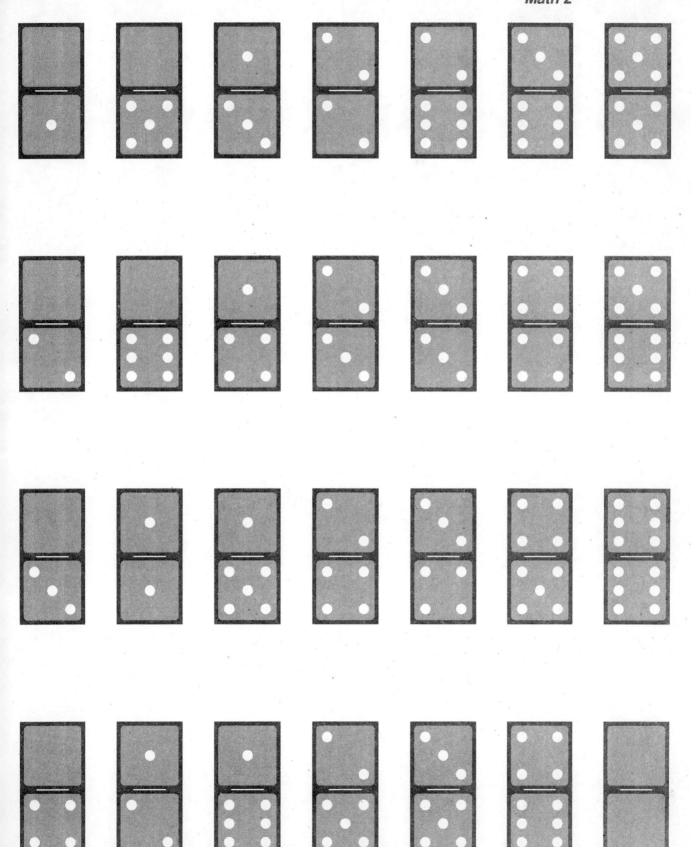

Domino Sums

								12
								11
								10
								9
								8
								7
								6
								5
								4
								3
								2
								1
								0

Domino Mix and Pick

12

11

10

9

8

7

6

5

4

3

2

1

0

$$\begin{array}{r} 4 \\ \times\ 4 \\ \hline \end{array} \qquad \begin{array}{r} 4 \\ \times\ 10 \\ \hline \end{array} \qquad \begin{array}{r} 1 \\ \times\ 4 \\ \hline \end{array} \qquad \begin{array}{r} 8 \\ \times\ 4 \\ \hline \end{array} \qquad \begin{array}{r} 4 \\ \times\ 3 \\ \hline \end{array}$$

$$\begin{array}{r} 4 \\ \times\ 5 \\ \hline \end{array} \qquad \begin{array}{r} 4 \\ \times\ 9 \\ \hline \end{array} \qquad \begin{array}{r} 6 \\ \times\ 4 \\ \hline \end{array} \qquad \begin{array}{r} 2 \\ \times\ 4 \\ \hline \end{array} \qquad \begin{array}{r} 4 \\ \times\ 7 \\ \hline \end{array}$$

$$\begin{array}{r} 0 \\ \times\ 4 \\ \hline \end{array} \qquad \begin{array}{r} 6 \\ \times\ 4 \\ \hline \end{array} \qquad \begin{array}{r} 4 \\ \times\ 4 \\ \hline \end{array} \qquad \begin{array}{r} 2 \\ \times\ 4 \\ \hline \end{array} \qquad \begin{array}{r} 4 \\ \times\ 9 \\ \hline \end{array}$$

$$\begin{array}{r} 4 \\ \times\ 7 \\ \hline \end{array} \qquad \begin{array}{r} 4 \\ \times\ 5 \\ \hline \end{array} \qquad \begin{array}{r} 4 \\ \times\ 1 \\ \hline \end{array} \qquad \begin{array}{r} 8 \\ \times\ 4 \\ \hline \end{array} \qquad \begin{array}{r} 3 \\ \times\ 4 \\ \hline \end{array}$$

$$\begin{array}{r} 4 \\ \times\ 10 \\ \hline \end{array} \qquad \begin{array}{r} 3 \\ \times\ 4 \\ \hline \end{array} \qquad \begin{array}{r} 4 \\ \times\ 5 \\ \hline \end{array} \qquad \begin{array}{r} 7 \\ \times\ 4 \\ \hline \end{array} \qquad \begin{array}{r} 4 \\ \times\ 0 \\ \hline \end{array}$$

Score: _____

$$
\begin{array}{r} 4 \\ \times\ 5 \\ \hline \end{array}
\qquad
\begin{array}{r} 2 \\ \times\ 6 \\ \hline \end{array}
\qquad
\begin{array}{r} 5 \\ \times\ 7 \\ \hline \end{array}
\qquad
\begin{array}{r} 6 \\ \times\ 10 \\ \hline \end{array}
\qquad
\begin{array}{r} 9 \\ \times\ 2 \\ \hline \end{array}
$$

$$
\begin{array}{r} 6 \\ \times\ 5 \\ \hline \end{array}
\qquad
\begin{array}{r} 10 \\ \times\ 9 \\ \hline \end{array}
\qquad
\begin{array}{r} 6 \\ \times\ 2 \\ \hline \end{array}
\qquad
\begin{array}{r} 2 \\ \times\ 4 \\ \hline \end{array}
\qquad
\begin{array}{r} 3 \\ \times\ 5 \\ \hline \end{array}
$$

$$
\begin{array}{r} 2 \\ \times\ 10 \\ \hline \end{array}
\qquad
\begin{array}{r} 2 \\ \times\ 7 \\ \hline \end{array}
\qquad
\begin{array}{r} 5 \\ \times\ 9 \\ \hline \end{array}
\qquad
\begin{array}{r} 10 \\ \times\ 8 \\ \hline \end{array}
\qquad
\begin{array}{r} 5 \\ \times\ 2 \\ \hline \end{array}
$$

$$
\begin{array}{r} 3 \\ \times\ 10 \\ \hline \end{array}
\qquad
\begin{array}{r} 5 \\ \times\ 5 \\ \hline \end{array}
\qquad
\begin{array}{r} 2 \\ \times\ 8 \\ \hline \end{array}
\qquad
\begin{array}{r} 5 \\ \times\ 1 \\ \hline \end{array}
\qquad
\begin{array}{r} 10 \\ \times\ 10 \\ \hline \end{array}
$$

$$
\begin{array}{r} 3 \\ \times\ 2 \\ \hline \end{array}
\qquad
\begin{array}{r} 0 \\ \times\ 5 \\ \hline \end{array}
\qquad
\begin{array}{r} 10 \\ \times\ 5 \\ \hline \end{array}
\qquad
\begin{array}{r} 8 \\ \times\ 10 \\ \hline \end{array}
\qquad
\begin{array}{r} 8 \\ \times\ 5 \\ \hline \end{array}
$$

Score: _____

Name •

(Draw a 9 cm line segment.)

Date •————————————•

(Measure this line segment using centimeters. _____ cm)

1. Each child in Mrs. Velardi's class has 3 pencils. There are seven children in the class. Draw a picture to show the children's pencils.

How many pencils do the children have altogether?

Number sentence _____ Answer _____

2. Use the Venn diagram to answer the questions.

Which letters on the graph
have only parallel line segments? _____

Which letters have
perpendicular line segments
but not parallel line segments? _____

Which letters have both parallel
and perpendicular line segments? _____

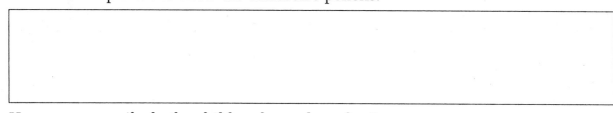

LETTERS

PARALLEL LINE   PERPENDICULAR LINE
SEGMENTS   SEGMENTS

M   E   T

N   F   I

Z   H   L

3. Round each number to the nearest 10 and add the rounded numbers.

57   +   12   43   +   21

_____ + _____ = _____   _____ + _____ = _____

4. Double the value of these coupons.

| 30¢ | _____ | 25¢ | _____

5. 8 dimes and 16 pennies = 9 dimes and _____ pennies

6. Find the answers.

```
  4 9 ¢        5 7 ¢      68¢ + 52¢ = _____      73¢ − 41¢ = _____
+ 3 3 ¢      − 2 9 ¢
```

Name _____

LESSON 131B

Math 2

Date _____

1. Eddie counted 6 cars. Each car has 4 wheels. Draw a picture to show the wheels on the cars.

How many wheels do 6 cars have?

Number sentence _____ Answer _____

2. Use the Venn diagram to answer the questions.

Which letters on the graph have perpendicular line segments but not parallel line segments? _____

Which letters have parallel line segments? _____

Which letters have both parallel and perpendicular line segments? _____

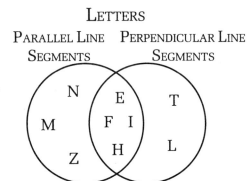

LETTERS

PARALLEL LINE   PERPENDICULAR LINE
SEGMENTS   SEGMENTS

3. Round each number to the nearest 10 and add the rounded numbers.

21 + 58

_____ + _____ = _____

38 + 18

_____ + _____ = _____

4. Double the value of these coupons.

50¢   _____

15¢   _____

5. 5 dimes and 18 pennies = 6 dimes and _____ pennies

6. Find the answers.

```
  5 4 ¢          8 5 ¢        47¢ + 28¢ = _____        91¢ − 36¢ = _____
+ 4 5 ¢        − 7 3 ¢
```

7 − 1	10 − 4	9 − 0	16 − 9	5 − 4	12 − 6	9 − 7	11 − 3	8 − 2	6 − 6
9 − 4	6 − 3	11 − 6	10 − 2	6 − 1	12 − 8	2 − 0	9 − 3	7 − 2	6 − 5
5 − 5	11 − 4	4 − 2	15 − 9	8 − 0	10 − 6	14 − 5	9 − 9	7 − 6	12 − 7
9 − 5	17 − 9	8 − 4	13 − 8	9 − 2	11 − 5	15 − 6	5 − 1	8 − 5	16 − 8
8 − 6	11 − 7	1 − 0	7 − 3	9 − 6	4 − 3	17 − 8	10 − 5	12 − 4	13 − 7
8 − 3	16 − 7	10 − 3	4 − 1	6 − 2	13 − 5	7 − 0	14 − 9	11 − 2	10 − 8
13 − 9	10 − 7	18 − 9	14 − 6	1 − 1	12 − 3	7 − 5	4 − 1	11 − 8	7 − 7
2 − 2	12 − 5	3 − 1	15 − 7	10 − 1	6 − 0	13 − 4	5 − 2	9 − 8	3 − 0
11 − 9	7 − 6	13 − 6	3 − 3	14 − 8	9 − 1	6 − 4	12 − 9	7 − 4	8 − 7
4 − 4	15 − 8	3 − 2	5 − 0	5 − 3	8 − 8	14 − 7	10 − 9	0 − 0	8 − 1

Name •

(Draw a 3" line segment.)

Date •————————————————•

(Measure this line segment using inches. _____ in.)

1. Each child at Kristina's birthday party ate 5 cookies. There were six children at her party. Draw a picture and write a number sentence to show how many cookies the children ate altogether.

Number sentence _____ Answer _____

2. Use the graph to answer the questions.

   How many children chose winter? _____

   How many more children chose spring than chose fall? _____

   Write two facts about the information on the graph.

   _____

   _____

   _____

CHILDREN'S FAVORITE SEASONS

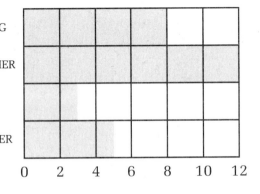

3. Write the answers.

   6 ÷ 2 = _____   18 ÷ 2 = _____   4 ÷ 2 = _____   12 ÷ 2 = _____

4. Pretend you are the teacher. Circle and correct the mistakes on this paper.

   1. Double this coupon. | 40¢ | 80¢

   2. Write August 8, 1994 using digits. 7/8/94

   3. Circle all the perpendicular line segments.

          ⊥   =   Ⓧ

   4. Round 37 to the nearest 10.   40

1. Each child at John's party drank 3 cups of juice. There were 7 children at John's party. Draw a picture and write a number sentence to show how many cups of juice the children drank altogether.

Number sentence _____ Answer _____

2. Ask 10 people their favorite season. (Color in $\frac{1}{2}$ of a box for every vote.)

How many people chose winter? _____

How many more people chose summer than chose winter? _____

Write two facts about the information on the graph.

_____

_____

_____

FAVORITE SEASONS

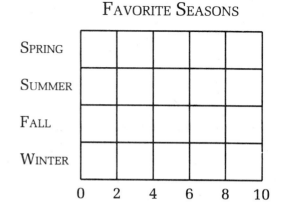

SPRING

SUMMER

FALL

WINTER

0   2   4   6   8   10

3. Write the answers.

8 ÷ 2 = _____   14 ÷ 2 = _____   10 ÷ 2 = _____   2 ÷ 2 = _____

4. Pretend you are the teacher. Circle and correct the mistakes on this paper.

> **1.** Double this coupon. | 15¢ | 35¢
>
> **2.** Write October 7, 1969 using digits. 9/7/69
>
> **3.** Circle all the parallel line segments.
>
>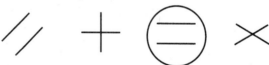
>
> **4.** Round 45 to the nearest 10. 40